The New JUMBO BOOK OF EASY CRAFTS

Written by Judy Ann Sadler

Illustrated by Caroline Price

Kids Can Press

To little crafters everywhere — *JAS*

Kids Can Press acknowledges the financial support of the Government of Ontario, through the Ontario Media Development Corporation's Ontario Book Initiative, and the Government of Canada, through the BPIDP, for our publishing activity.

Published in Canada by	Published in the U.S. by
Kids Can Press Ltd.	Kids Can Press Ltd.
29 Birch Avenue	2250 Military Road
Toronto, ON M4V 1E2	Tonawanda, NY 14150

www.kidscanpress.com

Edited by Lisa Tedesco and Sheila Barry
Designed by Kathleen Gray and Julia Naimska
Printed and bound in China

This book is limp sewn with a drawn-on cover.

CM PA 09 0 9 8 7 6 5 4 3 2 1

Library and Archives Canada Cataloguing in Publication

Sadler, Judy Ann, 1959–
    The new jumbo book of easy crafts / written by Judy Ann Sadler ; illustrated by Caroline Price.

ISBN 978-1-55453-239-1

1. Handicraft — Juvenile literature. I. Price, Caroline II. Title.

TT160.S235 2009	j745.5	C2008-903707-3

Kids Can Press is a *lorus*™ Entertainment company

Contents

☆ Make and Play 99

❋ Decorate and 139 Celebrate

Introduction

If you like to be creative and let your imagination go wild, then this is the book for you! *The New Jumbo Book of Easy Crafts* has over 150 fun, easy-to-make crafts just waiting to be discovered. The crafts are divided into four themed sections to help you find what you'd like to make. Let your artistic side take over in the **Imagine and Create** section where you'll learn to make creative clay, painted and printed pictures, paper strings and springs and over a dozen cute and silly animals. **Wear and Use** is filled with costumes and colorful jewelry to make and try on and lots of neat projects for your room. In **Make and Play** you'll have fun creating toys, games, puppets and musical instruments to share with your family and friends. And in **Decorate and Celebrate** you'll find ornaments, cards and flowers, gift bags and tags and many other great ideas to choose from to make your special days extra festive!

So what are you waiting for? Look through the color-coded sections, check the table of contents, flip to the index or open the book to any page and dive right in. It can be a sunny day, a rainy day, a weekday or a holiday — any day is perfect for making crafts! Before you know it you'll be happily snipping, coloring, twisting, gluing, rolling, painting, weaving, folding and decorating your way through this idea-packed book. Your home, classroom, dress-up box and toy cupboard will soon be filled with your creations. Enjoy!

Materials

You will find some crafty materials such as egg cartons, cereal boxes, scrap paper and plastic bottles around your home. Start by checking the recycling bin, but be sure to clean the items before you use them. Many other materials that you need are easily available at craft-supply, hardware and department stores. Use only non-toxic materials and keep scissors and small items such as beads and buttons out of the reach of babies and toddlers. Keep your craft supplies in a drawer, box or plastic bin so they are easy to find and ready to use. Adult supervision is always necessary when the instructions call for the use of an iron, stove or anything sharp. Wear an old shirt and cover your work surface with newspaper whenever you're using paint, glue or other messy materials.

Glue

Many crafts call for clear-drying, non-toxic, all-purpose craft glue. You can use a glue stick or hot glue gun (with adult supervision) as an option for some crafts.

Pipe cleaners

You will need pipe cleaners for some of the projects in this book. They are also known as "chenille stems" and are available in many colors, shapes and sizes. You can even get sparkly ones!

Cardboard

When a craft calls for "thin cardboard" this means cardboard from a cereal or cracker box. When you need "corrugated cardboard" this means cardboard from a packing box.

Supplies for decorating

For many crafts in this book, you'll need pencils, pencil crayons, crayons and markers. You will also need a few non-toxic permanent markers. Items such as stickers, glitter, ribbon, buttons, beads and feathers are great for decorating crafts, too.

IMAGINE and CREATE

Cooked play dough

This recipe makes a dough that you can play with over and over again. It can be rolled, sliced and molded into shapes, such as people, animals, food and flowers. Ask an adult to help you cook the dough.

1 In the pot, mix together the flour, salt and cream of tartar. Stir in water and oil.

2 Cook the mixture over medium-low heat, stirring constantly. When the mixture is thick and smooth, turn off the stove and remove the pot.

You will need

250 mL (1 c.) flour

125 mL (1/2 c.) salt

30 mL (2 tbsp.) cream of tartar

250 mL (1 c.) water

15 mL (1 tbsp.) cooking oil

food coloring

a pot and a spoon

plastic bags or tubs

3 Spoon the play dough out onto a counter that's dusted with flour. Allow it to cool for a few minutes.

5 Store each color of dough in a separate plastic bag or tub when you aren't playing with it, and it will keep for months.

4 Divide the dough into two or three balls. Knead a different food coloring into each ball until the color is even. (Or you can make all the dough the same color.) If the dough gets sticky, mix in a bit more flour.

Uncooked dough

This dough is fast and easy to make because it doesn't need to be cooked. It is best to use this dough for making stuff you want to harden and keep rather than for playing with over and over again.

You will need

250 mL (1 c.) flour

50 mL (1/4 c.) salt

125 mL (1/2 c.) water

food coloring

a bowl and a spoon

plastic bags or tubs

1 In the bowl, stir together the flour and salt and then add the water.

2 Mix the dough with your hands. If it does not hold together, add a little more water. If it is sticky, add a little flour. The dough is just right when it does not stick to your hands.

3 Divide the dough into two or more balls. Mix a few drops of food coloring into each ball. For a marbled look, mix the coloring in just a little.

4 If you are not going to use the dough right away, store it in separate plastic bags or tubs. It will last in the fridge for one to two weeks.

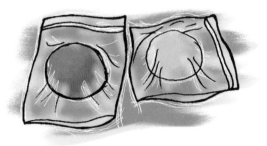

MORE IDEAS

Beads

Make beads by rolling some dough between your palms. Roll little beads between your index finger and thumb. Make holes in the beads with a straw, a pencil or a toothpick. (If you are going to bake your beads, make a large hole. The heat will puff up the beads and cause a small hole to close.) See below for how to finish your beads.

Fridge magnets

Pat some dough flat on a sheet of waxed paper. Press a cookie cutter into the dough and carefully lift off the cutout. See below for how to finish your magnet.

Finishing

To harden your beads or cutouts, place them on waxed paper to air-dry for a few days. Or place the beads and cutouts on a foil-lined cookie sheet and bake them in the oven at 120°C (250°F) for two to four hours. When the beads are dry, you may want to coat them with acrylic varnish or a Podgy-type product. To make the cutouts into fridge magnets, stick a magnet on the back of each one.

Cooked creative clay

The things you make with this clay will be hard, smooth and easy to paint. Ask an adult to help you cook the dough. If you'd like colored clay without painting it, add food coloring to the water before you mix it with the cornstarch and baking soda.

You will need

125 mL (1/2 c.) cornstarch

250 mL (1 c.) baking soda

175 mL (3/4 c.) water

food coloring (optional)

a small pot, a spoon and a bowl

a damp kitchen cloth

a plastic tub or bag

1 In the pot, mix together the cornstarch and baking soda and then add the water. Stir the mixture until it is smooth and no longer feels stuck to the bottom of the pot.

2 Cook the mixture over medium-low heat, stirring constantly. After a few minutes, it will start to thicken. When it looks like smooth, thick mashed potatoes, turn off the stove and remove the pot.

3 Spoon the ball of clay into a bowl. Cover the bowl with the damp cloth to cool.

4 When the clay is cool, knead it on a surface dusted with cornstarch. Knead in a little more cornstarch if the clay feels sticky.

5 Store the creative clay in a plastic tub or bag. It will keep for a couple of weeks in the fridge. Read on for what to make and how to finish your projects.

MORE IDEAS

See page 11 for how to make beads and fridge magnets. When they are dry, paint them with acrylic craft paint. Also, try the following ideas.

Ornaments
Roll out some clay on a sheet of waxed paper. If the dough sticks to the rolling pin, rub on a bit of cornstarch. Use cookie cutters to cut out shapes. Use a straw to poke a hole in the center top of each ornament. Leave the ornaments in a warm place to dry for a day or two, or bake them on a foil-lined sheet at 120°C (250°F) for a couple of hours. When the ornaments are hard and dry, paint them with acrylic craft paint. Thread a ribbon through each hole and hang up the ornaments. Or thread yarn or a long ribbon through the hole and wear an ornament around your neck.

Mobile
You could make a mobile by tying ornaments to criss-crossed sticks.

Frame
Make a mini frame by cutting out a large shape with a small shape cut out of the center. Paint and decorate the frame with buttons, beads or sequins. Tape or glue a photograph to the back.

Colored pasta

Try coloring many different types of pasta, such as macaroni, wagon wheels, rigatoni, tubetti and tubettini. Turn to page 60 to make pasta jewelry.

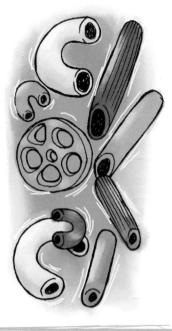

1 Spread a double thickness of newspaper over your work area.

2 Pour the food coloring and pasta into the plastic bag.

3 Twist the bag and hold it closed while you shake it.

4 Spread the pasta onto the newspaper. The newspaper helps to soak up the extra liquid.

You will need

newspaper

a small plastic bag

5 mL (1 tsp.) liquid food coloring

125 mL (1/2 c.) pasta

a spoon

waxed paper

plastic bags or tubs

5 Before the pasta begins to dry and stick to the newspaper, slide it onto a sheet of waxed paper. Use the spoon to spread out the pasta so none of the pieces are touching.

6 Let the pasta dry for about half an hour. This pasta is not for eating. Also, be careful not to get the pasta wet or the color may run.

7 Store colored pasta in plastic bags or tubs.

Squashed-paint pictures

Every time you make one of these pictures, it will be a one-of-a-kind work of art. Use a separate spoon or Popsicle stick for each color of paint you use.

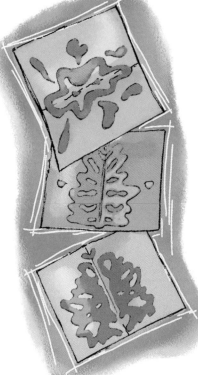

1 Cover your work surface with newspaper.

2 Fold a sheet of paper in half; open it again. Use a spoon or stick to dribble paint just along the fold, on one side only, or all over the paper.

3 Fold the paper in half and smooth it with your hands. Open it and look at your masterpiece!

You will need

newspaper

paper

plastic spoons or Popsicle sticks

acrylic craft paint

Dipped-string pictures

You can dip string directly into a small jar of paint or pour some paint out onto a pie plate. Use a separate string for each color of paint you use.

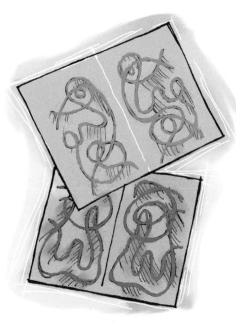

1 Cover your work surface with newspaper.

2 Fold a sheet of paper in half; open it again. Cut three lengths of string.

3 Dip each of the three strings into paint and place them any way you like on the right side of the paper. Refold the paper.

4 Press gently on the top of the folded paper and pull out the strings one at a time. Open your paper to see the designs you've created.

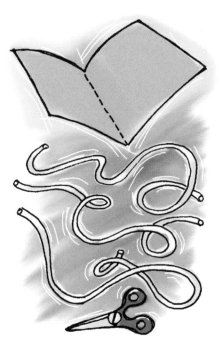

You will need

newspaper
a sheet of paper
scissors
string or yarn
acrylic craft paint

Crayon magic pictures

Use watercolor paints, such as the type you find in
a paint box, for this neat project.

1 Use the white crayon to
draw a picture on the paper.

2 Paint over it. The picture
will appear like magic!

You will need

paper

a white crayon

watercolor paint,
a brush and water

MORE IDEAS

Leave someone a mystery message by using a white
crayon on white paper. He or she will have to paint
the paper to get the message!

Instead of painting over paper with one color of paint,
use a rainbow of colors.

Rubbings

Look for textured surfaces and objects to rub. Try puzzle pieces, keys, coins, buttons, bark, leaves, shells and the bottom of your shoe.

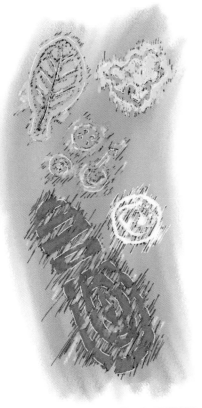

1 Hold the paper over the surface or object you wish to rub.

2 If the object is small, such as a coin, key or button, it's a good idea to hold it in place with a loop of tape on the back.

3 Rub the crayon over the paper and watch the design appear.

You will need

a sheet of paper
objects to rub
tape (optional)
crayons

Eraser prints

Use an art gum or white vinyl eraser for this project. Also try stamping with a new pencil eraser for a polka-dot design. For easy clean-up, it's best to use a washable ink stamp pad, but any type will do.

1 Press your eraser straight down on the ink stamp pad a few times. Stamp it on scrap paper to see what it looks like. Try other sides of the eraser, too.

2 Stamp on your good paper. Try to make interesting designs.

3 Before you use another color of ink on your eraser stamp, stamp it over and over on scrap paper to get rid of all the ink.

4 Use eraser stamps to decorate note paper, envelopes, posters, gift bags and other stuff.

You will need

an eraser
an ink stamp pad
scrap paper
paper

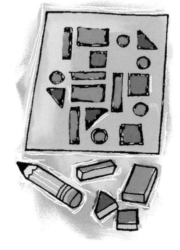

Thumbuddies

Use a stamp pad with non-toxic, washable ink so your hands don't get stained.

1 Press the pad of your thumb onto the stamp pad.

2 Press your thumb onto paper. Use a pen or marker to draw a face, arms and legs. You can add other features, too, such as a cane or a hat.

3 What other characters can you make? How about a row of fingerprints to make a caterpillar? Or a thumbprint and fingerprint for a butterfly body and you add the wings?

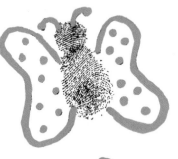

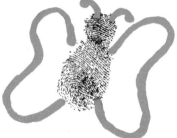

You will need

an ink stamp pad
paper
markers or a pen

Printmaking

Here are many great ideas for decorating posters, pictures, greeting cards, gift bags, wrapping paper and lots more. You will need acrylic craft paint, a paint tray, such as a foil pie plate, and a few more items described below. Have some scrap paper on hand to try out your printing ideas. If you'd like to print clothing, use fabric paint and see pages 64 and 65 for how to get ready.

Potato printing

Ask an adult to slice a potato in half and cut in a design, such as a flower, star, heart or geometric shape. Dip the potato in paint, test it and decorate your item. If you wish to change paint colors, rinse and dry the potato and dip it in the new color. You can cut and dip other vegetables and fruits too.

Handprints and footprints

You can place your open hand in paint and print it. Or try making a hand-footprint by printing the little-finger side of your fist. Make the toes by dipping your fingertips in paint and printing them. You can also dip an old running shoe into paint and "walk" it across your paper.

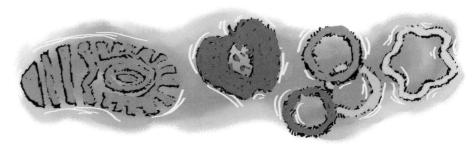

Dip, drizzle and splatter

Dip a Popsicle stick into paint and let it drizzle and drip onto your paper. Or dip the bristles of an old toothbrush into paint and, holding the bristles downwards, flick them with a Popsicle stick. Use lots of colors of paint.

MORE IDEAS

Dip any of the following items into paint and print with them: crumpled waxed paper, sponge shapes, pipe cleaners bent into designs or string glued onto a small block of wood.

Paper weaving

Once you've tried weaving, you'll want to do it often. Make the crafts listed in the more ideas box by following these instructions.

1 Fold one sheet of construction paper in half.

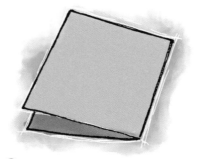

2 Starting at the folded edge, make cuts that end about two finger widths from the open edge. You can make the cuts wavy, straight or zigzag, and they can be different widths.

3 Cut 10 to 15 strips along the width of the second sheet. The strips don't need to be straight or even.

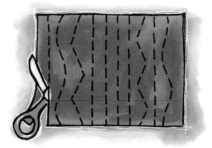

4 Open the first sheet of construction paper. Starting at one side, weave a strip of paper under and over the cuts in the construction paper. Slide the strip as far to one end as you can.

You will need

2 different-colored sheets of construction paper

scissors and all-purpose craft glue

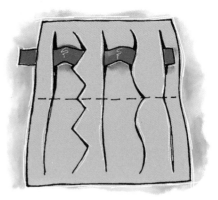

5 Weave in the second strip, with an over and under pattern opposite to that of the first strip. Push the second strip close to the first.

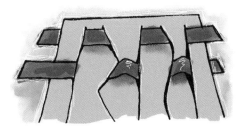

6 Continue weaving in strips until you run out of space. Glue down all the strip ends on both sides of the sheet.

MORE IDEAS

Placemat

Cover your weaving with clear self-adhesive vinyl (available at craft or hardware stores). Cut two pieces of vinyl a little larger than the weaving. Remove the paper backing from one piece and place it sticky side up on your table. Carefully set the weaving onto the vinyl. After removing the paper backing, place the second sheet of vinyl on the weaving and smooth both sides. Trim the vinyl all around if necessary.

Greeting card

Fold the weaving in half. Glue a sheet of paper inside to write on your greetings.

Rainbow weaving

Instead of using just one color for the strips, cut strips from many sheets of construction paper. You'll have rainbow weaving! Or, instead of construction-paper strips, use strips cut from wrapping paper or leftover wallpaper.

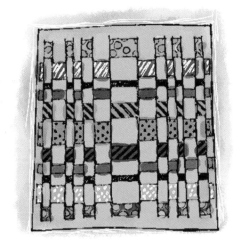

Fold-a-book

Take any sheet of paper and fold it into a book. You can fill yours with drawings, stickers, photographs or stories.

1 Fold your sheet of paper in half, open it and fold it in half the other way. Open it again. You've created two fold lines that look like a crisscross pattern.

2 Place the sheet of paper in front of you so that it is wider than it is tall. (If your paper is square, it doesn't matter which way you place it.) Fold the right side to the center fold line and then fold the left side to the center fold line. Open the paper again.

3 Fold it in half again on one of the first fold lines you made. (If you see three straight fold lines, fold it the other way so you see a crisscross fold pattern.) Cut the paper starting from the center of the folded edge to the middle fold line. Open the sheet of paper again.

4 Fold the sheet in half the opposite way, holding it so that the cut edge is at the top. Push the sides of the paper toward the center. You may need to gently pull apart the cut edges so that the paper can now be folded into a book.

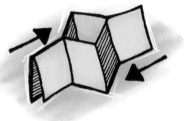

You will need

a sheet of paper, any size

scissors

Scrapbook

Make this scrapbook for cutouts, drawings, stickers and other stuff you wish to keep.

1 Cut two cardboard covers the same size as the sheet of construction paper.

2 Cover the printed sides of the cardboard covers with construction paper.

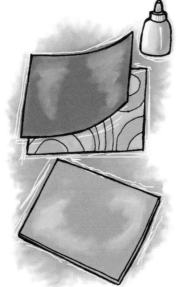

3 Ask an adult to help you hole-punch the covers with three holes each. Use them as a guide to hole-punch 10 or more sheets of construction paper.

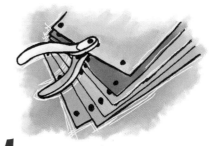

4 Fasten the scrapbook together with ribbon or rings. Decorate the cover.

You will need

thin cardboard (from a cereal box)

scissors, all-purpose craft glue and markers or crayons

construction paper

a hole punch

ribbon or binder rings

Construction-paper springs

Once you know how to make these springs, read on to create all kinds of neat stuff. The springs look great if you use two different-colored strips.

1 Use the ruler to draw two lines lengthwise on a sheet of construction paper. Cut out the strips. They should be about the same width.

3 Fold the vertical strip upward. Fold the horizontal strip over to the left.

4 Now fold the vertical strip down and the horizontal one to the right. Keep folding the strips together this way.

2 Glue the strips together to form a squared corner, as shown.

5 When you reach the end, glue the two ends together. Trim them if needed. Read on for fun projects to make with your springs.

You will need

a ruler

a pencil

construction paper

scissors

all-purpose craft glue or a glue stick

MORE IDEAS

You can use these springs for legs on animals, for bug-eyed paper monsters, to make a dress-up necklace and bracelet set and so much more.

Greeting card surprise

Fold two wide strips together. Glue one end of the spring inside a card you're making. Glue a heart, flower or message to the other end so it will jump out when someone opens the card.

"Spring" flower

Fold two different-colored strips together. When you finish, bring the two ends around to form a circle. Glue them together. Dab a little glue on the end of a pipe cleaner and poke it into one of the folds. Add pipe-cleaner or construction-paper leaves if you wish.

Caterpillar

Make an extra-long spring by taping strips together, end to end, before you begin folding. When your spring is finished, draw a face on one end. Add pipe-cleaner or construction-paper antennae.

Paper-doll strings

Try this with a regular sheet of paper first. Then try it with wrapping paper or newsprint from a roll.

1 Fan-fold your paper as shown, wide enough to draw a doll on it.

2 Draw on a doll shape making sure that at least the arms go off the edges of the folded paper.

3 With the paper still folded, cut out the doll shape. Unfold the string of dolls and color them in, if you like.

You will need

paper, a pencil and scissors

crayons or markers (optional)

MORE IDEAS

Try making strings of trees, hearts, eggs, bears — whatever you like. Just make sure that parts of the drawing go off the folded edges.

Penguin

Your penguin will look like it is waddling if you stand it up and gently rock it.

1 Trace part of a cup in one of the bottom corners of the envelope.

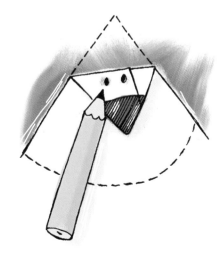

2 Fold over the tip of the corner to make the penguin's head. Draw on eyes and a beak.

3 Use a black crayon or marker to draw wings. Cut out the penguin.

4 Cut out a pair of rounded orange feet. Bend up the straight end and glue the feet in place.

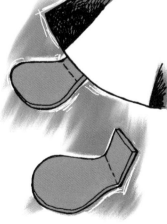

You will need

a white or light-colored used envelope

a cup

a pencil, scissors and all-purpose craft glue

crayons or markers including a black one

orange construction paper

Hand art

Do some hand art every year to keep track of how much your hands are growing! Send some hand art to Grandma and Grandpa so they can see how you've grown, too.

1 Place one hand on the paper. You can spread out your fingers a little or a lot or hold them close together.

2 Trace around your hand and cut the shape out.

3 Look at your cutout from all angles. Does it look like an animal? Could two hands together be butterfly wings? Antlers for a reindeer? Decide what to make. Draw on details with the markers. Write your name and the date on the back.

4 Try more hand positions for different pictures. You may want to decorate your hand by drawing on pretty jewelry and nail polish. Or make your hand scary!

You will need

construction paper

a pencil, scissors and markers or crayons

Going 'round in circles

Cut out oodles of different-sized circles, and glue them together to create as many animals as you can get around to making.

1 Trace lots of round items onto the construction paper. Cut out the circles.

2 Now start creating! Glue the circles onto a fresh sheet of construction paper and make different animals.

To make a caterpillar, glue many different-colored circles in a row, then draw on antennae, a face and feet.

For a ladybug, cut out a large circle for the body and a small circle for the head. Cut lots of wee circles for the ladybug dots. For the face, glue on beads or roly eyes and draw on a smile. Use a marker to draw a line down the center of the back for the wings.

You will need

round items, such as old bowls, cups and plastic lids

colorful construction paper

a pencil, scissors and all-purpose craft glue or a glue stick

markers or crayons

You can also try making a bear, mouse, poodle, turtle with a colorful shell or make up an original circle creature!

Wiggling caterpillar

You can use one color or many colors of construction paper for this cheerful caterpillar.

1 Trace four circles onto the construction paper. Cut them out.

2 Fasten the circles together in a row with the paper fasteners.

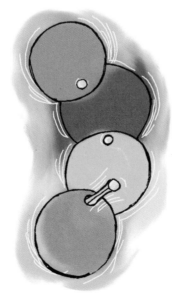

3 Draw a face on one end of the caterpillar. To make antennae, poke in the pipe cleaner ends from the back to the front and curl the ends.

4 Tape a Popsicle stick to the back of the head and tail circles. Push the sticks together, then pull them apart to make the caterpillar move and wiggle.

You will need

a cup or lid to trace

construction paper

a pencil, scissors, tape or all-purpose craft glue or a glue stick

paper fasteners

crayons or markers

a short pipe cleaner

2 Popsicle sticks

Hatching-egg surprise

See if your family or friends can guess what will hatch from this big egg!

1 Draw a large egg on a sheet of construction paper. Cut it out.

2 Cut the egg in half by making a jagged line. Poke a hole in a corner of each half of the shell and hold the halves together with a paper fastener.

3 On a different color of paper, draw the top half of a chick, bird, lizard, snake, turtle or dinosaur. Draw on a face and cut it out.

4 Glue the creature to the bottom half of the shell so its head and neck are showing. When you close the shell, you should not be able to see what's inside.

You will need

a pencil, scissors and all-purpose craft glue or a glue stick

construction paper

a paper fastener

crayons or markers

Fly-away ladybug

Make this ladybug any two colors you like. If you use black for the head, use a white crayon, acrylic paint, beads or roly eyes to make the face.

1 For the bug's body, trace a circle onto a piece of construction paper. Draw a round bump on it for the head. Cut out the head and body.

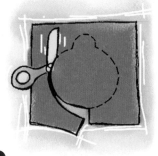

You will need

colorful construction paper

cups or lids to trace

a pencil, scissors and all-purpose craft glue or a glue stick

crayons or markers

a paper fastener

2 For the wings, trace a larger circle, fold it in half and cut it along the lines.

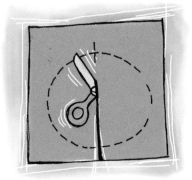

3 Draw ladybug spots on the wings or cut out dots and glue them on.

4 Slightly overlap the top of the wings and poke the paper fastener through them. (You may need to poke in a pencil hole first.) Fasten the wings to the neck area. Draw on a face.

Movable fuzzy bear

After you've made this fuzzy bear, try making a bunny with long, movable ears or a dog with a wagging tail.

1 Glue the felt to the sheet of paper.

2 On the paper side, draw four chubby legs, an oval body and a round head with ears. Cut out all six parts.

3 Use the scissors to carefully cut or poke small holes into one end of each leg and the chin area of the head. Poke holes in the body and attach the head and legs with the paper fasteners.

4 Draw on a face and claws.

You will need

paper, a pencil, scissors and all-purpose craft glue

a square of felt

5 paper fasteners

markers

Cotton-ball sheep

Try this method to make other animals, too — such as bunnies or chicks.

1 Slightly stretch out a cotton ball. You'll find it stretches out more easily one way than the other. Glue it on the paper.

2 Draw on legs, a tail and a head. Make more sheep.

3 If you like, you can create a whole scene. Add cotton-ball clouds and draw on more details, such as shrubs and grass.

you will need

cotton balls
construction paper
all-purpose craft glue
markers or crayons

MORE IDEAS

Snow scene

Create a snowy landscape. Use two or more cotton balls to make a snowman. Draw on details. Pull apart cotton balls to look like snow on the ground. Roll up bits of cotton for snowflakes falling from cotton-ball clouds.

Cotton-ball trim

Draw a picture of a person. Glue on cotton-ball hair or a cotton-ball mustache and beard. Also, draw a hat and glue on fluffy, white trim. Use cotton balls on masks and costumes, too.

Pom-pom bear

You may want to use a few different colors of pom-poms for this fuzzy bear.

1 For the head and body, glue the medium pom-pom to the large one.

2 Glue a medium-small pom-pom to the face to make a muzzle. Glue on the other four medium-small pom-poms for legs.

3 Glue on two small pom-poms for ears and one for the tail.

4 Glue on the roly eyes and a bead nose.

You will need

a large pom-pom

a medium pom-pom

5 medium-small pom-poms

3 small pom-poms

all-purpose craft glue

2 roly eyes

a small bead

Striped snake

If you don't have narrow ribbon, you can use yarn, embroidery floss or other thin, strong cord. You can use different colors than the ones in these instructions.

1 Thread a green bead onto the ribbon so it hangs in the center.

2 Hold both ribbon ends together and thread on a pink bead, a green bead, a pink bead and so on until you have about ten of each color.

3 To make the head, separate the ribbon ends and thread three green beads onto each end.

4 Knot the ribbon ends together to hold on the beads. Trim them to look like a snake's tongue. Draw on eyes.

You will need

about 50 cm (20 in.) of narrow red ribbon

wooden or pony beads in pink and green

scissors

a non-toxic permanent marker

Button puppy

Who would have thought that you could make a funny little puppy character out of buttons and beads?

You will need

a pipe cleaner

scissors

a small bead

a big bead with a large hole

8 medium or large buttons

a scrap of felt or construction paper

all-purpose craft glue

a non-toxic permanent marker

1 Cut the pipe cleaner in half. Cut one of the pieces in half again. Set aside the two short pieces.

2 Thread the small bead onto the center of the long piece of pipe cleaner. (If the bead does not fit, use a bead with a larger hole.) Bend the pipe cleaner in half.

3 Poke both ends of the pipe cleaner into the big bead, and slide it up to the small bead. This makes a muzzle and head.

4 Thread one of the buttons onto the pipe-cleaner ends. (If your button has four holes, thread the pipe-cleaner ends through two diagonal holes.) Wind one of the short pipe cleaners behind the button to create the front legs.

5 Thread on six more buttons. Then wind on the other short pipe cleaner to make the hind legs.

6 Thread on the last button. Twist together the ends of the pipe cleaner to keep the buttons in place and to create a tail.

7 To make paws, fold over the end of each pipe-cleaner leg.

8 Cut small ears out of felt or paper and glue them to the sides of the puppy's head. Now draw on a face.

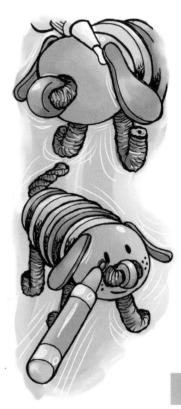

Beady spider

Not even Little Miss Muffet would be afraid of this cute spider!

1 Cut the pipe cleaners in half. Twist the pieces together in the center. Spread some glue on the center area.

3 Thread small beads onto each leg and bend the end over to hold the beads in place.

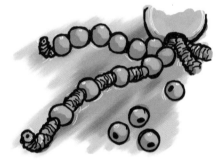

You will need

2 pipe cleaners

scissors

2 large beads with large holes

white craft glue

small beads

markers or paint and a brush

2 Thread a large bead onto the pipe-cleaner legs until it reaches the glue in the center. Spread the legs out.

4 Glue on the second large bead for a body and a small bead for a nose, as shown. Draw or paint on eyes, a mouth and interesting markings.

Crazy-eight octopus

You won't believe how fast you can make this interesting octopus.

1 For the legs, make eight evenly spaced cuts two-thirds of the way up the roll.

2 Bend and curl the eight legs so they are spread out.

3 Draw on a face and markings.

you will need

*a cardboard roll
scissors
crayons or markers*

Cardboard roll creatures

There are many creatures you can make. All it takes is a cardboard roll and your imagination. These instructions are for making a bunny.

1 Cut a strip of construction paper big enough to wrap around the roll. Glue it in place.

3 Draw on a face and glue on a tiny pom-pom nose if you have one.

You will need

a cardboard roll

construction paper

scissors and all-purpose craft glue or a glue stick

crayons or markers

a tiny pom-pom (optional)

a cotton ball or pom-pom

2 Cut the roll in half. (You'll need to shape the pieces so they are round again.) Glue the two halves together as shown.

4 Cut out long ears from more construction paper. Glue them in the space between the two halves of the roll.

5 Cut out feet and glue them under the head.

6 Glue on the cotton ball or pom-pom tail.

MORE IDEAS

Make other animals by changing the colors of the construction paper and the shape of the ears, tails and paws. Poke in pipe cleaners for legs, antennae or a curly tail. Use yarn for a mane or a long tail. Try sitting your animal upright. If your creature falls over, glue it to a small cardboard base.

Egg-carton caterpillar

There are many ways to decorate this cheerful caterpillar. You can paint it, color it with markers and crayons or use stickers.

1 Cut out one of the rows of egg cups from the carton.

2 Decorate the caterpillar any way you'd like. Draw on a face.

3 Use the pencil, nail or needle to poke two holes into the top of the head egg cup.

4 Bend the pipe cleaner in half. From underneath, poke one end into each hole in the egg cup. Curl the pipe-cleaner ends into antennae.

You will need

a clean cardboard egg carton

scissors

a pencil, a nail or a blunt needle

a 15 cm (6 in.) pipe cleaner

a marker or crayon and other decorating supplies

Egg-carton raccoon

This raccoon is a funny little character with his black mask and ringed tail.

1 Cut an egg cup out of the center area of the carton rather than one of the corners.

2 Trim off any ragged edges, but otherwise leave the cup as it is. It should have three scooped-out sides and one straight one. The straight side will be the raccoon's backside.

3 On the front, draw ears, a nose, whiskers and a black mask-like area where the eyes will go. Draw lines on the paws. Glue the beads in place for eyes.

4 Cut a tail from the egg-carton lid. Draw stripes on it and glue it to the raccoon's backside.

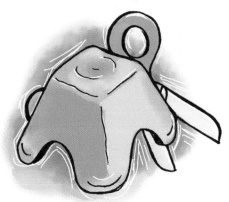

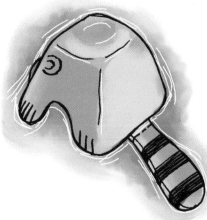

You will need

a clean cardboard egg carton

scissors

a black marker

beads or roly eyes

all-purpose craft glue or a glue stick

Ladybug

After you've made this charming bug, try making lots of other colorful critters. You could make a spider with eight black pipe-cleaner legs.

1 Cut an egg cup out of the carton. Trim it so it is smooth and straight all around.

2 Color or paint the egg cup red.

3 Draw or paint on a face, spots and a line down the center of the ladybug's back.

4 Make three small holes on each side of the cup. Poke a piece of pipe cleaner into a hole on one side and out the hole straight across on the other side. Make the other legs the same way.

You will need

a clean cardboard egg carton

scissors

crayons, markers or paint and a brush

a pencil, a nail or a blunt needle

a pipe cleaner cut into 3 pieces

Egg-cup chick

These chicks are so cute, you'll want to make a dozen of them!

1 Cut two egg cups out of the carton. Trim them so they are smooth and straight all around.

2 Color or paint them both yellow or any color you like.

3 To make a beak, fold the scrap of paper in half and cut a triangle on the fold. Place it between the cut edges of the cups and glue the cups together.

4 Draw on eyes. Make a hole in the back of the top cup. Poke in the tail feather.

You will need

a clean cardboard egg carton

scissors and all-purpose craft glue

crayons, markers or paint and a brush

a scrap of construction paper

a pencil, a nail or a blunt needle

a colored craft feather

Dragonfly

Use bold colors to decorate this neat dragonfly.

1 Color the clothespin with paint or markers. Or leave it the original color and just draw on markings.

2 To make wings, wrap one of the pipe cleaners around the middle of the clothespin and twist it twice. Shape each half of the pipe cleaner into a long, narrow wing and fasten its end to the center area. Repeat this with the other pipe cleaner.

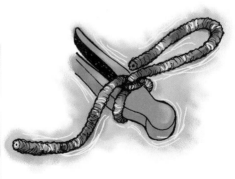

3 Glue the beads to the head for eyes. Allow them to dry.

4 Cut a length of fishing line and tie it around the dragonfly. Hold the dragonfly up by the line to see if it is balanced. Adjust the line, if necessary, and knot it in place. Hang up your dragonfly.

You will need

a flat craft clothespin

markers or acrylic craft paint and a brush

2 pipe cleaners

2 round beads

scissors and all-purpose craft glue

fishing line, thread or yarn

Gazelle

Some gazelles have long, straight, ringed horns. This makes it easy to create a model gazelle from clothespins.

1 On one of the clothespins, draw fine lines across the two ends to make horns.

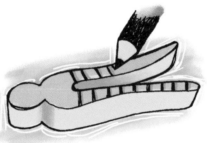

2 Glue together the other two clothespins. Now glue the head to the legs as shown.

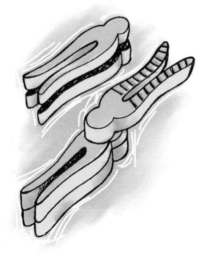

3 Cut out ears and a short tail from the felt or construction paper. Glue them in place.

4 Use roly eyes, beads or markers for the face. Draw on hooves.

You will need

3 flat craft clothespins

markers

scissors and all-purpose craft glue

beads or roly eyes (optional)

a scrap of felt or construction paper

Rock painting

Many rocks look like ladybugs, turtles or other creatures. Some are perfect for painting on scenes. What does your rock look like?

1 Pick up a stone and look at it from all different angles. Does it look like a car? A bug? An animal curled up sleeping?

2 Paint the rock any way you like. You can even swirl different colors of paint together to give it a marbled look. Place it on waxed paper to dry.

3 If you'd like your rock to shine, coat it with varnish.

You will need

interesting rocks

acrylic craft paint and a brush

waxed paper

acrylic varnish (optional)

Stone writing

When you're at the beach, look for many small, smooth, flat stones for these magnetic message rocks.

1 Write something on each stone. If you write a letter of the alphabet on each one, you can put them together to make words. If you write words, you can make sentences. Or write on numbers or the names of special people and places.

2 Cut pieces of the magnetic strip and press them to the backs of the stones.

3 Leave someone a message on the fridge.

You will need

clean, flat stones

non-toxic permanent markers

self-sticking magnetic strip

scissors

Rocky puzzle

Find a handful of rocks and pebbles to make a unique rock puzzle. These instructions are for a person, but you could make animals, a tiny town or a rock band!

1 Choose a round rock for the head and an oval rock for the body. Find narrow stones for the arms and legs and small round ones for the hands. See if you can find small, oval stones for the shoes. Can you find a stone for a hat?

2 Draw or paint on a face, hair, clothing and shoes.

3 Place all the rocky puzzle pieces into the plastic bag. See if your brother, sister or friend can put it together.

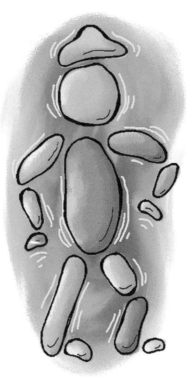

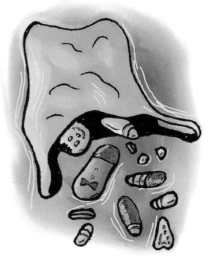

You will need

an assortment of rocks

non-toxic permanent markers or acrylic craft paint and a brush

a small plastic bag

Rocky bee

Place this bee in a bouquet of flowers you've made from page 142 or 143. Or place it in a bouquet of real flowers.

1 Color the stone yellow. Allow it to dry.

2 Paint or draw on black stripes and a face.

3 Wrap a pipe cleaner around the center of the stone and twist it twice on top. Shape each half into a wing and fasten them at the center.

4 Wrap a second pipe cleaner around the center, and twist it on the underside. Use these ends to hold up the bee in a vase of flowers. (If the pipe cleaners don't stay in position, you may need to apply some glue.)

You will need

a light-colored, oval stone

yellow and black acrylic craft paint and a brush or non-toxic permanent markers

2 pipe cleaners

all-purpose craft glue (optional)

Acorn-head doll

For the stuffing, use crumpled paper, felt scraps or a part of a clean rag. If you include some potpourri with the stuffing, your doll will smell sweet.

1 Trace the plate onto the felt and cut it out.

2 Gather the felt circle around the stuffing. Twist it closed with the pipe cleaner.

3 Trim the pipe cleaner and bend the ends to look like arms and hands.

4 Squirt glue into the center of your doll's gathered neck and sit the acorn on it. Let it dry, then give your doll a face. If you like, remove the cap from the acorn, glue on some yarn hair and glue the cap back in place.

You will need

a lunch plate

a square of felt

a pencil or pen, scissors and all-purpose craft glue

stuffing

a pipe cleaner

an acorn

markers, paint and a brush or other supplies for the face

yarn (optional)

WEAR and USE

Pasta jewelry

For making a pasta bracelet, use elastic thread or cord. For making a necklace, garland or mobile, try waxed dental floss, waxed linen, fishing line, embroidery floss or heavy thread.

1 Cut a piece of elastic thread about three times the length around your wrist or as long as you'd like for a necklace.

3 Thread on pasta. If you are using elbow macaroni, a neat squiggly pattern will form. Trim the end of your thread if it frays.

2 Tie a piece of small pasta near one end of your thread so the others won't fall off. (You may want to remove it when your jewelry is finished.)

4 When your jewelry fits, triple knot the ends together.

you will need

elastic thread or cord

scissors

colored pasta
(see pages 14 and 15)

Beaded jewelry

By using elastic thread for this bracelet, necklace or anklet, you do not need a clasp.

1 Cut a length of elastic thread about 30 cm (12 in.) long for a bracelet or anklet or at least 75 cm (30 in.) long for a necklace.

2 Thread on a bead and tie it near the end of the elastic thread.

3 Thread on more beads. If your elastic thread frays, trim off the end and keep going.

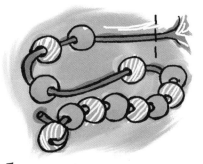

4 Try on your piece of jewelry. Take off or add on beads until it fits. Tightly knot the ends together.

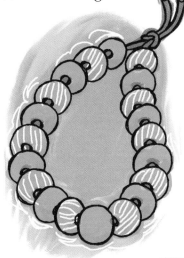

You will need

elastic thread or cord

scissors and a ruler

a variety of beads

Drinking-straw beads

To make these beads, you can use leftover pieces of wrapping paper, colorful magazine and catalog pages, construction paper or any other scrap paper.

1 You can use a pencil and ruler to mark straight lines for cutting, or simply cut strips of paper. The strips can be as wide or narrow as you'd like your beads to be.

2 If your strips are long, cut them into pieces about 8 cm (3 in.) long.

3 Begin winding one end of a strip of paper onto a straw. Spread a little glue on the paper as you go.

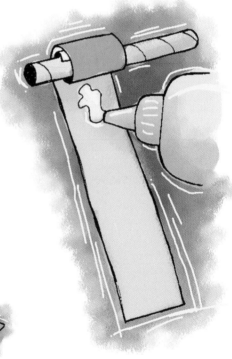

You will need

paper

scissors, a ruler, a pencil and all-purpose craft glue or a glue stick

drinking straws

4 When you are near the end, spread a little more glue on the strip, then finish rolling it. Hold the paper for a moment while the glue dries.

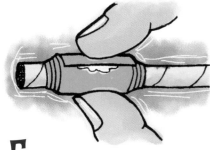

5 Slide the bead off the straw, or cut off the straw on each side of the bead. Make lots more beads!

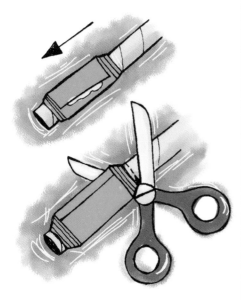

MORE IDEAS

Wind more than one color of paper to make a bead. Begin with a wide strip. When you finish rolling it onto a straw, dab a bit of glue on it and wind a narrower strip around it. Add a third or fourth layer if you wish.

Cut long triangles of paper. To make the beads, wind the wide end of a triangle around the straw. Guide the paper as you roll so the point of the triangle ends up in the middle of the bead.

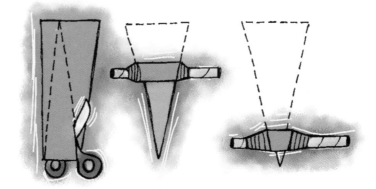

If you'd like shiny beads, coat them with acrylic varnish or a sealer product, such as Podgy or Mod Podge, while they're still on the straws.

Thread your beads onto elastic cord, plastic lace or yarn to make a necklace or a bracelet.

Fabric-paint fun

When you decorate clothing, use fabric paint. Try some of the printmaking ideas from pages 22 and 23 or use dimensional fabric paint (it comes in small, squeezable bottles) to draw on designs.

1 Your article of clothing should be washed, dry and smooth. You don't need to wash shoes and laces, and only wash your hat if it is washable and likely to be washed often.

2 Here's how to prepare different articles of clothing for printing.

- Put cardboard in between the two layers of fabric for a shirt, shorts, a jacket, socks or gloves.

- Remove the laces from shoes and fill the toes with crumpled paper.

You will need

an article of clothing such as a T-shirt, a hat, gloves, socks or shoes and laces

cardboard, scrap paper, tape and a bowl (see step 2)

fabric paint

printing supplies

• Tape the ends of shoelaces to your work surface.

• Stuff a hat with crumpled paper or place it over an upside-down bowl.

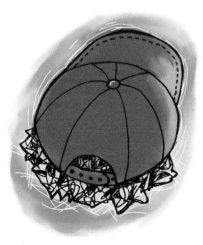

3 Test your designs on scrap paper first, then print or draw designs on your article of clothing.

4 When your article of clothing is dry, you need to set the paint. Cover the printed area with a clean cloth and have an adult iron it on a hot setting for two minutes (or follow the paint manufacturer's instructions). You do not need to set the paint for items that will not be washed or if you used dimensional fabric paint.

Animal ears

Try making pig, cat, dog, bunny and bear ears using this simple method. They're great for dress-up, plays or just for fun.

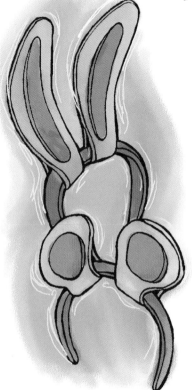

1 Fold the felt in half. Cut out two ears so the base of each ear is along the fold.

2 Unfold the ears and spread glue over the inside of each.

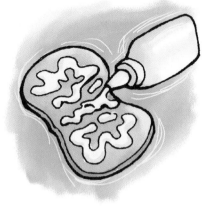

3 Fold the ears back in half, this time around the hair band.

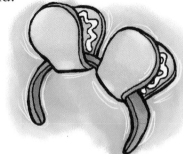

4 Use the paper clips to hold the ears together close to the hair band. Remove the paper clips when the glue is dry.

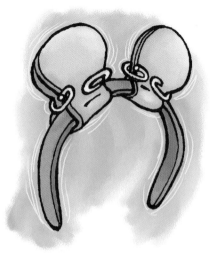

You will need

a square of felt

scissors and all-purpose craft glue

a hair band

paper clips

Antennae

Use any combination of colors for the hair band, pipe cleaners and pom-poms. If your hair band is smooth, you may need to add tape to hold the pipe cleaners in place.

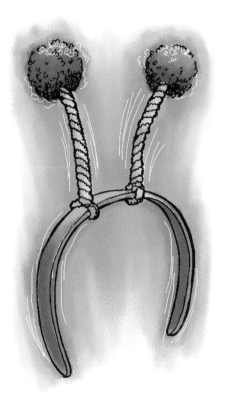

1 Twist the center of one pipe cleaner firmly around one of the pom-poms.

2 Twist the pipe-cleaner halves together almost to the ends. Fasten the ends to the hair band, making sure the tips of the pipe cleaners end up on top of the band so you don't get poked.

3 Follow steps 1 and 2 for the other antenna. Fluff the pom-poms so you can't see the pipe cleaners wound around them.

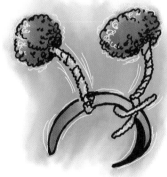

4 Curve the antennae (or zigzag them) and try them on.

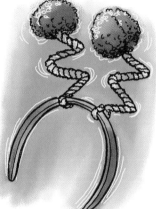

You will need

2 pipe cleaners
2 pom-poms
a hair band

Frog eyes

Use store-bought green pom-poms for this craft.

1 Glue the pom-poms a little way apart on the top of the hair band. It is helpful to place the hair band against a book (or something similar) while the glue dries.

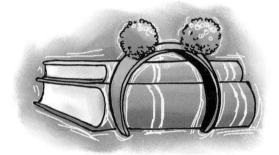

2 Cut out two small circles from the cardboard. Draw on large black dots.

3 Glue the circles to the front of the pom-poms. Allow the glue to dry. Try on your frog eyes. Ribbet!

You will need

a hair band

2 large pom-poms

all-purpose craft glue and scissors

thin cardboard (from a cereal box)

a pencil, markers or crayons

Dress-up braids

Find some old, clean pantyhose or tights for this braided wig. You can use three different-colored pantyhose or three the same color.

1 On one of the pairs of pantyhose, make a short cut on each side of the center seam in the crotch area.

2 On the other two pairs of pantyhose, cut off the top part above the legs so the legs are still connected.

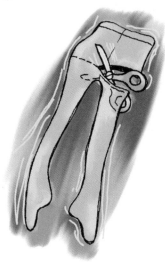

3 Hold the two trimmed pairs of pantyhose together and pull them through the slits in the first pair. All three crotch areas should end up together.

4 Braid each side. Fasten the ends with a rubber band and trim the ends if they are uneven. Tie bows over the bands if you like.

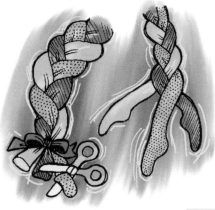

You will need

3 pairs of pantyhose or tights

scissors

2 rubber bands

ribbon (optional)

No-sew dress-up cape

You can buy felt by the meter (or yard) at a fabric or craft-supply store.
Decorate your finished cape with dimensional fabric paint or any fancy trim.

1 Fold over and pin about 5 cm (2 in.) of the felt along one of the long sides.

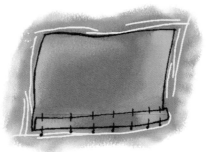

2 Cut short slits all along this folded edge about every 5 cm (2 in.). Remove all the pins and unfold the felt.

3 Weave a length of ribbon in and out of the slits and gather the felt to look like a cape. Knot a ribbon end into the first slit on each side of the cape to keep the ribbon from being pulled out.

4 Try on the cape. Trim the bottom edge so you don't trip on it. Make it jagged for a witch's cape, wavy for a princess or straight for a superhero.

You will need

1 m (1 yd.) of felt
a ruler and scissors
straight pins
ribbon

Royal crown

By using a paper clip to hold this crown together, you can adjust the size. When the clip is removed, the crown is flat and easy to put away.

1 Draw a crown shape onto the cardboard. Cut it out.

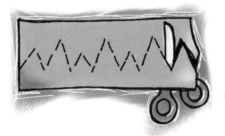

2 Spread glue on the cardboard. Place it glue side down on a strip of fabric or felt. Allow the glue to dry.

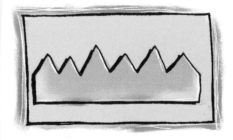

3 Cut out the fabric or felt around the crown. Glue on rhinestones, sequins, lace or other trim.

4 Try on the crown and hold it together with one or two paper clips.

you will need

a pencil, scissors and all-purpose craft glue

thin cardboard or poster board, about 64 cm (25 in.) long

plain fabric or felt

supplies for decorating (see step 3)

1 or 2 large paper clips

Goofy glasses

These glasses may not help you to see better, but they're a fun dress-up accessory.

1 Shape two of the pipe cleaners into big circles by twisting their ends together. Wrap the fastened area with tape so there are no sharp ends.

3 Bend the other two pipe cleaners in half. Fasten one on the side of each circle. Twist the arms and curve the ends to fit around your ears. Wind tape around the ends and try on your glasses.

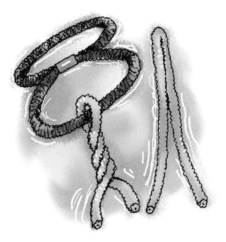

2 Place the circles side by side and tape them together as shown.

You will need

4 pipe cleaners

cloth or masking tape

Tin-can stilts

It's best to use these outside, but if that isn't possible, use them inside on carpet. Use cans from apple juice, coffee or canned tomatoes.

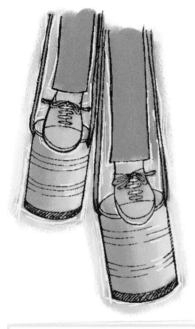

1 Tape around the rim of the open end of each can. (If there are jagged edges, you may need to tap them down with a hammer first.)

2 On the closed end of each can, position the can opener so that it cuts a triangular hole on the side rather than the top of the can. Make another hole across from the first.

3 Cut two pieces of twine a little longer than you are tall. Thread each end of twine into one of the holes in each can from the outside to the inside. Tightly knot the ends together inside the can.

4 Wear rubber-soled shoes on the stilts so you don't slip off. Grip the ropes, keep your arms and legs straight and start walking. If the ropes are too long (they should be about as high as your mid-thigh) shorten them by re-knotting them in the can.

You will need

2 same-sized, clean tin cans, open on one end only

cloth or masking tape

juice can opener

twine, cotton rope or heavy jute

scissors

Jester hat

This felt project (along with the collar on page 75) can also be put together by an adult using a hot glue gun.

1 Place one of the felt squares on the table in front of you. Fold it in half from left to right. Place the ruler diagonally from the bottom right-hand corner to the top left-hand corner and draw a line. Cut along the line. Unfold the felt. Repeat this for the other felt square so that you now have two tall triangles.

3 Turn the hat right side out and glue a pom-pom onto the tip. Or you can ask an adult to help you stitch on a large jingle bell.

4 Try on your jester hat. Roll up the edge until it fits well.

You will need

2 squares of felt in different colors, 45 cm x 45 cm (18 in. x 18 in.)

a ruler, pencil or fabric marker and scissors

fabric glue or tacky glue

a large pom-pom or jingle bell

2 Glue the triangles together along their two long edges. Allow the glue to dry.

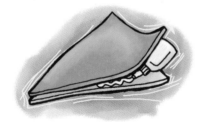

Jester collar

You can buy a large piece of felt at a fabric store.

You will need

a strip of felt, about 120 cm x 15 cm (48 in. x 6 in.)

a ruler

a few paper clips

scissors

small colorful pom-poms or different-colored scraps of felt

fabric glue or tacky glue

a length of satin ribbon about 100 cm (40 in.) long

1 Fold over about 2.5 cm (1 in.) along one long side of the strip of felt and hold the fold with paper clips. Cut short slits along the folded edge about every 4 cm (1 1/2 in.). If there isn't one there already, cut an extra slit 1 cm (1/2 in.) in from each end.

2 If you are not using pom-poms, cut out shapes, such as circles, diamonds or hearts, from the scraps of felt. Glue these shapes or the pom-poms onto the strip of felt, being sure not to cover any of the slits you've just made. Allow the glue to dry.

3 Starting at one end, weave the ribbon in and out of the slits. Gather the collar into ruffles along the ribbon. Try on the collar and adjust the ruffles, then knot the ribbon through a slit at each end. Leave the ribbon tails so you can tie the collar around your neck. Put on a large shirt and the hat from page 74, and you'll have a great court jester costume.

Top hat

If you use the same color of ribbon on this hat as you use to decorate the stick on page 77, you'll have a matching top hat and walking stick.

1 Cut a strip of board 60 cm (24 in.) long and 14 cm (5 1/2 in.) wide. Measure and mark a line 1 cm (1/2 in.) in along one of the long edges.

You will need

a ruler, pencil, scissors and all-purpose craft glue

a sheet of poster board (also called bristol board)

a stapler (optional)

a length of wide satin ribbon

2 Roll the strip into a cylinder and try it on. Adjust the hat to fit your head, take it off and glue or staple the ends together.

3 To make the brim, stand the top of the hat on the poster board and trace it. (Make sure it stays round in shape, not oval.) Remove the top of the hat, and measure and mark another circle 8 cm (3 in.) outside of the first circle. Cut out the brim along the outside circle. Carefully poke your scissors into the center circle and cut it out, too. Set aside the brim.

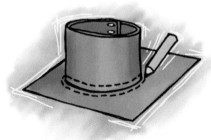

4 Make small cuts about 1 cm (1/2 in.) apart up to the line on the top of the hat that you marked in step 1. Bend the tabs. This is the edge that will be glued to the brim of the hat.

5 Slide the brim over the top of the hat and glue the tabs to it. Glue the ribbon around the hat. If you like, you can gently curve up the sides of the brim.

Walking stick

To make this walking stick you can use a dowel, a cylindrical or rounded length of wood, or try a smooth branch instead.

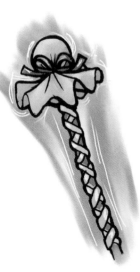

You will need

a length of wooden dowel, about half your height and 1.5 cm (5/8 in.) in diameter

acrylic craft paint, a brush and water (optional)

tape or all-purpose craft glue

1 or 2 ribbons, each 30 cm (12 in.) longer than your stick

duct tape

a circle of felt, 20 cm (8 in.) in diameter

a rubber band

another length of ribbon 50 cm (20 in.) long

1 If you like, you can paint the wooden dowel. Allow it to dry.

2 Tape or glue one end of a piece of ribbon to the top of your stick. Wind it down the length of the stick and then fasten it at the bottom. If you are using a second ribbon, wind it in the opposite direction.

3 Cut a piece of duct tape and wad it into a small ball. Tape it to the top of the stick.

4 Cover the tape ball with the circle of felt and fasten it in place with the rubber band. Tie a length of ribbon over the rubber band.

Magic wand

Find a stick and transform it into a magic wand!

1 Draw a star (it doesn't have to be perfect) on one of the sheets of foam and cut it out. Use it as a pattern to trace and cut another star on the same foam. Use one of these stars as a guide to draw a slightly larger star on the other color of foam. Cut out the large star.

2 Bend the pipe cleaner in half. Using two or three staples, fasten the bent end of the pipe cleaner to the center of the large star.

3 Glue a small star onto each side of the large one so that the staples and the bent end of the pipe cleaner are covered. You may wish to place a heavy book on the stars while the glue dries.

4 Spread glue around one end of the stick. To fasten on the star, wrap the ends of the pipe cleaner through the glue. Bend the pipe cleaner so that the star is straight. Allow the glue to dry. For decoration, tie ribbons around the pipe cleaner and curl the ends.

You will need

2 different-colored sheets of craft foam

a pencil, scissors and all-purpose craft glue

a pipe cleaner

a stapler

a stick about 30 cm (12 in.) long

curling ribbon

Fleecy fringed poncho

These instructions will show you how to make a small poncho, but if you'd like to make a larger one, simply use a bigger fleece square.

You will need

a 75 cm x 75 cm (30 in. x 30 in.) square of Arctic Fleece or Polarfleece

scissors

a pencil or fabric marker

a ruler or measuring tape

1 Place the square of fleece on a table so that it is in a diamond shape. Fold the top point down to the bottom point, then fold the left side over to the right side. Cut off a small piece of fleece at the tip of the upper left-hand corner.

2 Unfold the fleece from right to left so that you have a large triangle. Measure and mark a point 18 cm (7 in.) from one side of the small hole. Poke your scissors into the hole and cut a slit to the mark you just made.

3 Try pulling the poncho over your head. If it doesn't fit, remove the poncho and cut the slit slightly longer. When it fits comfortably, cut around the edges of the slit so that the opening looks like a long, thin teardrop.

4 To add fringe, make cuts about 5 cm (2 in.) deep and 1 to 2 cm (1/2 to 3/4 in.) apart around the edge of the poncho. At the corners, cut out small squares of fleece where the cuts from two sides meet.

79

Tissue-paper lei

For this lei, you can use store-bought beads as well as straw beads (see page 62) and pasta beads (see pages 14 and 15). Aloha!

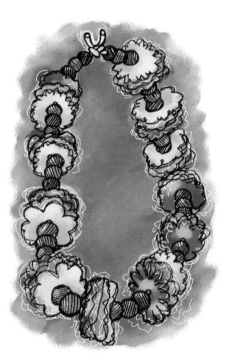

1 Cut out many tissue-paper flowers in lots of colors, shapes and sizes.

2 Thread at least two arm lengths of yarn into the needle. Make a knot in the long end of the yarn.

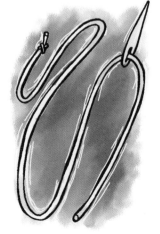

3 Thread on a couple of beads, tissue flowers, more beads, more flowers and keep going.

4 When your lei is long enough to fit easily over your head, knot the yarn together and trim the ends.

You will need

colorful tissue paper

scissors

yarn and a blunt needle with a large eye

small beads

Leggy neck roll

You can use an old pair of jeans, pajama pants or sweat pants to make this easy neck roll pillow. Make a whole pile of pillows for a cozy reading corner.

1 Use pinking shears to cut off one pant leg 50 cm (20 in.) or more from the bottom hem. (If you don't have pinking shears, use regular scissors, then run a bit of glue around the cut edge to keep it from fraying.)

2 Tightly knot ribbon, yarn or cord around one end of the leg about 8 cm (3 in.) from the end.

3 Roll up the old towel or sheet so that it fits nicely into the leg tube, leaving enough space for the leg to be tied closed. (If you are using regular stuffing, tightly fill the leg.)

4 Tie the other end of the leg closed. If you like, you can jazz up your neck roll by knotting extra lengths of ribbon around the ends.

You will need

an old pair of pants

pinking shears

thick satin ribbon, heavy yarn or cord

a ruler

an old towel, bed sheet or stuffing

Fridge magnets

Make lots of magnets using many colors and shapes of foam.

1 Draw a shape on a foam sheet. Try a flower, a heart or an animal.

2 Cut out the shape. If you have another color of foam, glue the shape onto it. Cut around the shape so both colors show.

3 If you wish, you can write a message on the foam with a pen.

4 Cut a piece of magnetic strip, peel off the paper backing and press the magnet onto the back of the foam shape. Stick your finished magnet on the fridge.

You will need

craft foam

a pencil, scissors and all-purpose craft glue

a pen (optional)

self-sticking magnetic strip

Button frame

Instead of decorating this frame with buttons, you can use shells, sequins, lace, ribbon or beans. If you are framing one of your own drawings, be sure to date and sign it.

You will need

a picture

a piece of corrugated cardboard larger than your picture

a pencil, a ruler and all-purpose craft glue

construction paper

buttons or other decorating supplies

1 Place your picture on the cardboard. Decide how much of a frame you'd like around it. Draw lines using the ruler as a guide. Cut out the cardboard frame. (Do not cut out the center area.)

2 Trace the cardboard onto construction paper. Cut out the construction paper and glue it onto the cardboard.

3 Glue your picture in the center. Glue buttons all around it. Let the glue dry.

4 For a stand, cut a strip of cardboard almost as tall as the frame. Fold it about one-third from the top, and glue the bent part to the center top area of the back of the frame.

Jar-lid frame

What a fun and easy way to make a small picture frame!
Make lots so that you can line your shelves and windowsills
with framed photos and drawings.

1 Trace the lid on an area of a photograph or drawing that you'd like to frame.

2 Cut out your picture inside the pencil lines and glue or tape it to the inside of the lid.

3 To make a stand, cut a strip of cardboard about 3 cm (1 1/4 in.) wide and almost as tall as your lid. Fold over about 2.5 cm (1 in.) of the cardboard at one end, and tape or glue the folded part to the back of the lid frame.

4 If you like, you can glue beads, ribbon or other decorative trim around the outside of the frame.

You will need

a clean plastic lid, such as one from a jar of mayonnaise

a photograph or drawing

a pencil, scissors, ruler and all-purpose craft glue or tape

a scrap of cardboard

beads, ribbon or other trim (optional)

Stick frame

For this natural-looking frame, gather dry, fallen sticks
and twigs small enough to break with your hands.

1 Cut a piece of cardboard a little longer and wider than your photograph or drawing. Cover the cardboard by gluing on construction paper.

2 Break two twigs a little longer than the sides of the cardboard. Glue them to the sides so they stick out beyond the cardboard on each end.

3 Break two twigs a little longer than the ends of the cardboard. Glue these twigs to the other twigs so they cross at the four corners of the cardboard.

4 Glue the photograph or drawing to the center of the frame. Allow the glue to dry.

5 To stand the frame up, cut a strip of cardboard almost as high as the frame. Fold it about one-third of the way from the top. Glue the bent part to the center top area of the back of the frame.

You will need

scissors and all-purpose craft glue

corrugated cardboard

a photograph or drawing

construction paper

twigs

twine or ribbon (optional)

Popsicle-stick basket

If you have colored sticks, you can use them. If you don't, you can color them with paint or markers or leave them plain.

1 On a sheet of waxed paper, line up about 10 sticks, side by side.

2 In the opposite direction and evenly spread apart, glue four sticks to the first layer. Make sure each stick is glued to all 10 sticks under it. After it dries, flip it over.

3 Now build the sides of the basket. First, glue a stick on each side, then on the top and bottom. Alternate between the sides and the top and bottom until the basket is as tall as you want. Let it dry.

4 For the handle, fasten on a pipe cleaner.

You will need

Popsicle sticks
waxed paper
all-purpose craft glue
a pipe cleaner

Woven berry basket

Do you have a stack of empty plastic berry baskets kicking around? Jazz them up with colorful ribbon or fabric strips.

1 Cut or tear strips of ribbon or fabric long enough to go a little further than once around the outside of the basket. Cut enough strips to cover your basket.

2 Weave the first strip in and out of the openings of the basket. When you get back to where you started, keep weaving until the end of the strip overlaps with the beginning.

3 Continue weaving the other strips until your basket is covered. Trim off any extra ribbon or fabric, and snip off any frayed threads.

4 When you're finished weaving the first basket, decorate the other baskets in the same way. If you like, you can fasten the baskets together in a row or group with pipe cleaners, or you can make pipe-cleaner handles. If you want to put small items in the baskets, line the bottoms with felt.

you will need

1 or more clean plastic berry basket(s)

ribbon or cotton fabric

scissors

pipe cleaners (optional)

felt (optional)

Decorated basket

Transform a cardboard fruit basket into a terrific toy-carrier or gift basket.

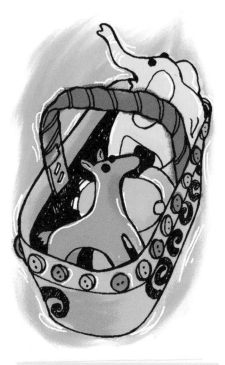

1 If you are going to store small items, such as buttons and beads, in your basket, smoothly tape over the corner openings on the inside and outside.

2 Paint the basket all one color. Allow it to dry.

3 Paint on designs, such as stripes, swirls or flowers. Or glue on buttons, beads or other small, interesting items. You can wrap yarn, ribbon or strips of fabric around the handle.

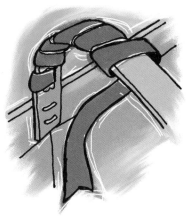

You will need

a clean fruit basket

tape (optional)

acrylic craft paint and a brush

buttons, all-purpose craft glue, beads, yarn, ribbon, fabric or other decorating supplies (optional)

MORE IDEAS

Art caddy

Place yogurt cups and other plastic containers
in your decorated basket and fill them with crayons,
markers, pencils, stickers and other craft supplies.
Leave enough space for a small pad of paper. Now
you can be creative everywhere you go!

Baby doll bed

Place a piece of felt or soft fabric, such as fleece,
in the bottom of the basket. Use a bandanna, felt or
fleece for a blanket. Give your doll something to play
with by tying a small plastic toy from the handle of
the basket. You can decorate another basket to carry
doll clothes, bottles and other accessories.

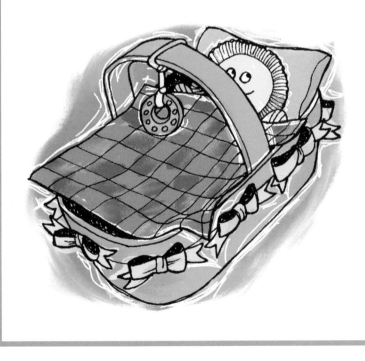

Wagon train

This train is perfect for holding your stuffed animals and other toys.

You will need

2 or more shoeboxes

a large nail

a pencil or pen, scissors and a ruler

supplies for decorating (see step 2)

cord, ribbon or twine

a big bead with a large hole

1 If your shoebox has a flip-top lid, cut it off. Stand the box on one end on a carpeted floor, and use the nail to start a hole near each of the two top corners. Turn the box around and do the same on the other end. Make the holes a little larger by poking in a pencil or pen. Prepare the other shoebox(es) in the same way.

2 Here are some ideas for decorating the inside and outside of your shoeboxes:

- Glue on magazine pictures or wrapping paper
- Draw pictures on the boxes with markers or crayons
- Glue on construction paper, and then add stickers, beads, buttons or ribbon

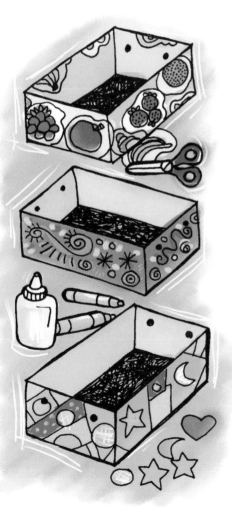

3 To fasten two boxes together, cut two pieces of cord, ribbon or twine, each about 20 cm (8 in.) long. Thread the end of one of the cords through a hole in the back of one box and tie it with an overhand knot to hold it in place. Thread the other end through the same-side hole in another box and knot this cord end in place, too. Fasten together the boxes on the other side as well. If you have more than two boxes, fasten the others together in the same way.

4 Decide which is the front of your wagon train. Cut a 90 cm (36 in.) length of cord. Starting from the outside, thread one end of the cord into one hole and out the other, then thread both ends of the cord through the bead. Knot the ends together to hold the bead in place.

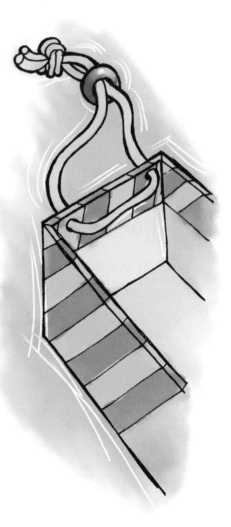

Piggy pot

This decorated clay pot can hold crayons, markers, wrapped candies, keys or a small plant. After making this piggy pot, try a bear or puppy pot.

1 Glue on the eyes and button nose.

2 Draw on a mouth and cheeks with markers.

3 Cut out two diamond-shaped felt ears. Glue them to the inside top rim of the pot and flip them over the edge to the outside. Glue them down on the outside top rim, too.

4 Coil the pipe cleaner by wrapping it around a pencil. Glue the pipe cleaner to the back of the pot for a tail. (If it won't stay in place, tape it until the glue dries.)

You will need

a medium-sized clay pot

a pair of small beads or roly eyes

a 2-hole button

a pencil, scissors, all-purpose craft glue and markers

scraps of felt

a short pipe cleaner

Decorated pot

If you like, you can paint the pot with acrylic craft paint before you begin gluing on decorations.

1 Wrap the ribbon around the top rim of the pot and tie it in a bow. You may wish to dab glue on the bow to keep it from coming undone later. Trim the ends of the ribbon.

2 Glue pretty buttons or beads around the pot. Or glue many of them in a design, such as a flower or heart. Allow the glue to dry.

You will need

a clay pot, any size

a ribbon

an assortment of buttons and beads

scissors and all-purpose craft glue

MORE IDEAS

Use sponge shapes dipped in acrylic craft paint to decorate a pot. Or glue small cut pieces of tissue paper, wrapping paper or fabric all over it.

Envelope bookmark

Here's a great way to recycle used greeting-card and junk-mail envelopes.

1 Fold the scrap paper in half. Along the fold line, draw and cut out half a medium-sized heart.

2 Open the heart and place it so its point is in one of the bottom corners of the envelope. If the heart is too large for the envelope, fold the heart again and trim it.

3 Trace the curved parts of the heart (lobes) onto the envelope. Write on a message, such as "I love reading," "Hold my spot" or "I was here."

4 Cut out the heart. To use it, open it and slide it over the top right-hand corner of the page you'd like to mark.

You will need

scrap paper
a pencil and scissors
a used envelope
markers or crayons

Braided bookmark

This whimsical bookmark will make you smile every time you open your book. Happy reading!

1 Cut 12 pieces of yarn, each about 40 cm (16 in.) long. Hold the pieces of yarn together so that the ends are roughly even. Bend the pipe cleaner in half and poke it into the bead. Thread the yarn through the looped end of the pipe cleaner. Pull it through the bead. Remove the pipe cleaner and pull one end of the yarn through.

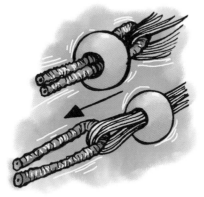

2 Tie an overhand knot in the yarn about 2.5 cm (1 in.) from one end. Pull the bead up to the knot. Make another knot below the bead.

3 Tape the bead to the edge of your table. To make arms, separate three strands of yarn on one side of the bundle of yarn, and braid them until you get halfway down the length of the yarn. Knot the yarn and trim off the extra strands. Repeat this step for the other arm.

4 To make the body of the bookmark, braid the rest of the yarn together. Knot it at the end. Remove the tape and draw a face on the bead.

You will need

yarn

a ruler and scissors

a pipe cleaner

a big bead with a large hole

masking tape

a non-toxic permanent marker

Paper-plate clock

Here's a great way to practice telling time.

1 Flip over the paper plate. Draw the numbers on the clock, beginning with "12" and "6," then "3" and "9."

2 Use the scissors to poke a hole in the center of the clock.

3 For the hands, cut two strips of cardboard, one shorter than the other. Round off one end of each and cut the other end into a point. Punch a hole in each rounded end.

4 Use the paper fastener to tightly attach the hands to the clock face.

You will need

a paper plate

a pencil, crayons or markers

scissors

thin cardboard (from a cereal box)

a hole punch

a paper fastener

Hang-ups

Make many hang-ups to string from doorways and windows, or use them as garlands to decorate an archway or tree.

1 Draw a shape, such as a star, flower, heart, circle, square or diamond, onto the thin cardboard. Cut it out and use it as a pattern to trace and cut many copies of the same shape out of paper.

2 Cut a length of yarn about 25 cm (10 in.) longer than you'd like your hang-up to be.

3 Place a cutout shape on your table and spread glue on it. Lay the cut yarn across the shape, leaving a tail about 25 cm (10 in.) long above the shape. To create a loop, double back the end of the tail into the glue. Firmly smooth a second shape on top of the first one.

4 Continue gluing the rest of the shapes together, each time catching the yarn in between. Trim off any extra yarn at the end of your hang-up.

Doorknob hanger

Turn your day-and-night doorknob hanger to the moon before you go to bed and to the sunny side when you wake up.

You will need

a large jar lid or small bowl to trace

3 sheets of thick paper or construction paper: one black, one light blue and one yellow

a pencil, scissors and all-purpose craft glue

crayons, including one that is white or light-colored

a hole punch

a piece of ribbon or yarn

1 Trace a circle on the black paper and another one on the light blue paper. Cut out the circles and glue them together. Punch a hole near the edge.

2 Draw a banana-shaped moon on the light blue paper and cut it out. Draw and cut out a sun shape from the yellow paper.

3 Glue the moon on the black circle and draw on a sleepy face. Use a light-colored crayon to draw stars around the moon. Glue the sun on the blue circle and draw on a smiling face.

4 Thread a ribbon through the hole, knot it and hang up your new doorknob hanger.

MAKE and PLAY

Tissue-box dollhouse

This dollhouse is made from empty tissue boxes. Begin with two rooms and add more when you have other empty boxes.

1 Cut the tops off the boxes.

2 Use the paper clips to fasten the boxes together side by side or end to end.

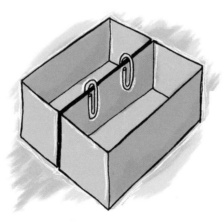

3 Make doorways between the rooms by cutting out pieces of the boxes. (You will need to unfasten the boxes to cut along the bottom edges.)

4 Create an outside door by making a cut down the side of one of the boxes. Also cut it across the bottom edge to the size you want. Fold back the door so it looks hinged.

You will need

2 or more empty tissue boxes

large paper clips

scissors

catalog pictures, all-purpose craft glue and other craft supplies (see step 5)

5 Now comes the fun part — decorating the rooms! Here are some ideas:

• Paint the walls or paste on construction paper, fabric or leftover wallpaper.

• Use fun fur, felt, fleece or carpet scraps for floor coverings.

• Decorate wooden blocks to make dressers, counters or a TV.

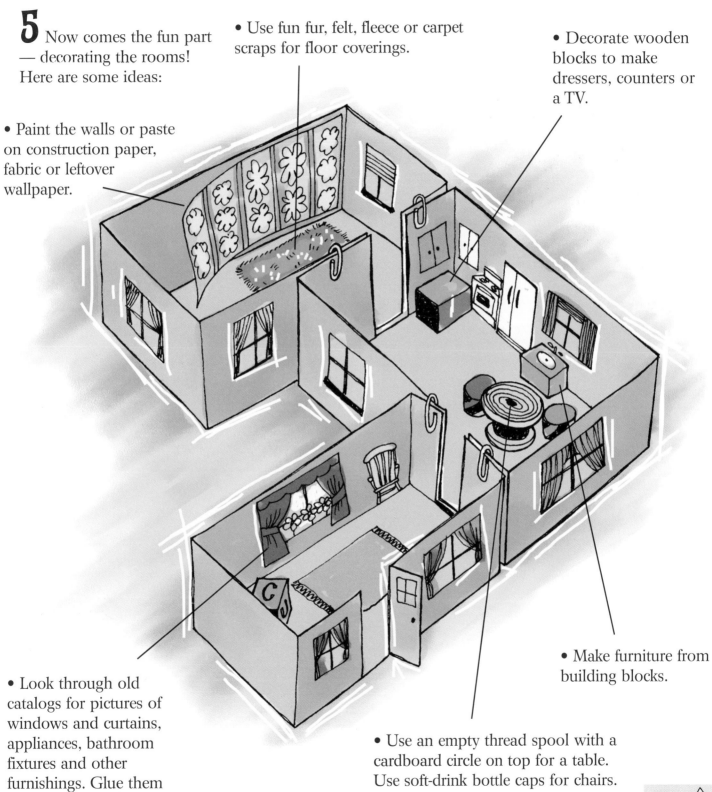

• Look through old catalogs for pictures of windows and curtains, appliances, bathroom fixtures and other furnishings. Glue them to the walls.

• Use an empty thread spool with a cardboard circle on top for a table. Use soft-drink bottle caps for chairs.

• Make furniture from building blocks.

Flower fairy

To make it look as if your flower fairy is flying, hang her up with clear nylon thread or fishing line.

You will need

2 pipe cleaners

a large colorful button

a large round bead

scissors

a few small beads with large holes, such as pony beads

a silk flower

a non-toxic permanent marker

a 20 cm x 20 cm (8 in. x 8 in.) square of craft netting, thin fabric or tissue

scraps of yarn

a tinsel pipe cleaner

1 Fold one of the pipe cleaners in half, and thread on the button by poking a pipe-cleaner end into each button hole. (If your button has four holes, thread the pipe-cleaner ends through two diagonal holes.) Slide the button up to the folded end. This is your fairy's hat.

2 Thread the round bead onto both ends of the pipe cleaner and slide it up to the hat.

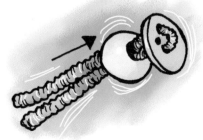

3 Cut the other pipe cleaner in half. Set aside one half. To make arms, wrap the other half around the folded pipe cleaner just below the head.

4 Thread on the pony beads and slide them up to the arms.

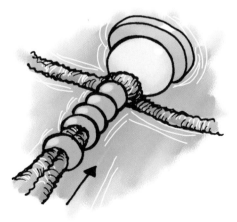

5 Remove the head of the silk flower from the stem. There should be a hole in the center. Thread the flower (whole or in layers) onto the pipe-cleaner legs and slide it up to the beads.

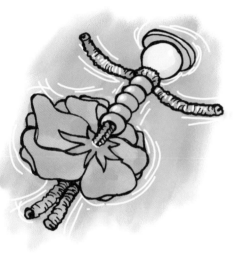

6 Fold over each of the four pipe-cleaner ends, then bend them up to look like hands and feet.

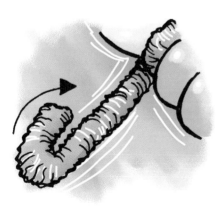

7 Draw a face on your flower fairy.

8 For the wings, fold the craft netting in half one way and then the other. Use the other half of the pipe cleaner to fasten the layers together in the center. (Cut open the layers if you like.) Attach the wings to your fairy by wrapping the ends of the pipe cleaner around the fairy's neck or the upper part of her body.

9 To make hair, cut three strands of yarn and tie them tightly under your fairy's button hat. You can style the hair by braiding, twisting or unraveling the yarn.

10 Bend part of the tinsel pipe cleaner into a magic wand. Trim off the rest. Fasten the wand into your fairy's hand.

Bead buddies

These instructions are for making one bead buddy, but by using beads in a variety of colors, shapes and sizes, you can create dozens of different buddies.

You will need

1 1/2 pipe cleaners

a large button

a large bead

small and medium-sized beads

yarn

scissors

paint and a brush or non-toxic permanent markers

1 Fold the long pipe cleaner in half and thread on the button. This is the hat.

2 Thread the large bead onto both ends of the pipe cleaner and slide it up to the hat.

3 For the arms, place the short pipe cleaner between the folded one, just below the large head bead.

4 Thread a few beads with large holes up both pipe-cleaner legs to make the body.

5 Separate the legs and thread on beads. Leave enough space on the ends to make small loops. Bend them up to look like feet.

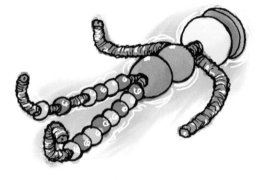

7 Cut two or three strands of yarn for the hair. Tie the yarn under the button hat. Style the hair by braiding, twisting or unraveling it.

6 Bead the arms, too, leaving enough space to make loops for hands.

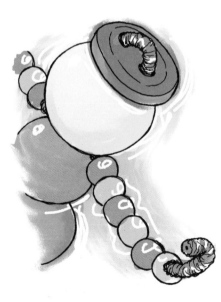

8 Draw or paint on a face. Name your new buddy!

yarn friend

To make this doll, choose a hardcover book that is as tall as you'd like your yarn friend to be.

1 Wind yarn around the book — about 20 times for very thick yarn and 50 times for regular yarn. Cut the yarn end.

2 Cut an arm's length of yarn. Slide the wound yarn off the book and tie it together at the top with the cut piece of yarn. Knot the tying yarn ends together to make a loop.

3 Tie another piece of yarn a little lower down to make a head. Let the yarn ends hang down the back.

4 Cut all the looped ends at the bottom of the doll.

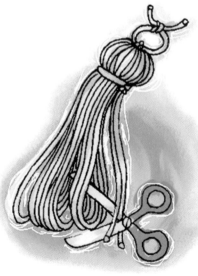

You will need

a hardcover book

yarn

scissors

roly eyes, beads, felt or other decorating supplies

5 Separate some strands of yarn from the doll's sides to make arms. Tie the strands in an overhand knot and trim off the extra yarn.

7 Leave the rest of the yarn hanging loose for a skirt or separate it into two legs. Tie them at the feet. Trim off any uneven strands of yarn.

6 Tie the waist with another piece of yarn and let the ends hang down the back.

8 If you'd like to make hair, tie a few strands of yarn around the long loop on your doll's head. Create a face. Hang up your yarn friend or use the loop to make it into a marionette.

Clothespin flyer

You will need a clothespin with a spring for this airplane.
The propeller really spins! You can color the airplane with markers
or paint after you've put it together.

You will need

a scrap of thin cardboard

scissors, an eraser and all-purpose craft glue

a straight pin

a spring-action clothespin

4 Popsicle sticks

1 Cut a small propeller from the cardboard. It can be straight or propeller-shaped.

2 Place the propeller on the eraser. Have an adult poke into the propeller's center with the pin. Wiggle the pin in the propeller hole to make it bigger.

3 Squeeze the clothespin open and spread glue on the open, inside area. Place the pin in the glue and close the clothespin. Adjust the pin so the propeller can spin freely.

4 Glue two of the Popsicle sticks to the upper side of the clothespin and allow the glue to dry. Glue two more sticks to the under side. Allow the glue on all parts of the airplane to dry completely.

Clothespin pal

You'll want to make a whole gang of these! For a puppet, leave off the stand and glue a stick between the legs.

1 Draw pants, a shirt and shoes on the clothespin. You can color just the front or all around the clothespin. Draw on a face, too.

2 Wrap the pipe cleaner around the waist for a belt. Twist it twice at the back and bring the ends to the front for arms. Fold over the tips of the pipe cleaner to make hands.

3 Cut a few pieces of yarn for hair. Spread glue on top of the head and place the yarn in it. If the yarn hair is long, you may wish to style it.

4 To make a stand, cut a strip of thin cardboard about 18 cm (7 in.) long. Fold it in half and place it between the legs. Bend the ends upward so your clothespin pal can stand.

You will need

a flat craft clothespin

markers and all-purpose craft glue

a short pipe cleaner

yarn

thin cardboard

Plastic-bag parachute

Make a clothespin pal (see page 109) to go with this fun and easy parachute. Be sure to stay away from trees and overhead wires when you play with your new parachute toy.

1 From the bag, cut a piece of plastic at least 35 cm (14 in.) square.

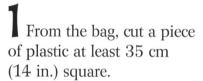

2 Smooth the plastic square on your table. Use the markers to draw on stars, squiggles, flags, stripes, your name or anything else.

3 Cut four pieces of yarn each 60 cm (24 in.) long.

4 Use the pencil to poke a hole in each corner of the plastic (but not too close to the corner edges). Knot a piece of yarn in each hole.

You will need

a plastic bag

scissors, a ruler and a pencil

non-toxic permanent markers

yarn

a clothespin pal or a small plastic toy

5 Hold the four yarn ends together and fasten them in an overhand knot as shown.

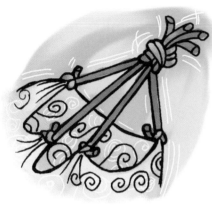

6 Loop the yarn around your clothespin pal's pipe-cleaner arms (or fasten it to a plastic toy).

7 To prepare your parachute for skydiving, hold it by the center of the plastic so the strings and pal hang down. Fold over the parachute and loosely wind the strings and pal around it to make a small bundle.

8 Toss up the parachute bundle as high as you can. It will float gently to the ground.

Weather chart

You can also use this felt board for other felt figures and shapes that you have made or bought. Large pieces of felt are available at fabric and craft-supply stores.

1 Glue together two pieces of cardboard, each about the size of a cookie sheet. (You may need to put heavy books on top to keep them flat.)

2 Spread glue over one side of the cardboard and smooth a piece of felt over it.

3 Cut out felt weather symbols, such as clouds, a bolt of lightning, raindrops, an umbrella, a sun, snowflakes and a bent-over tree or wavy grass for wind. You can use permanent markers to add detail if you like.

4 Check the weather and place the proper symbols on your weather chart.

You will need

corrugated cardboard

all-purpose craft glue and scissors

felt

non-toxic permanent markers (optional)

Wind sock

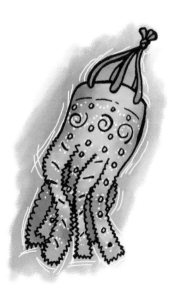

For this project, it's good to use ripstop fabric because it's thin and strong and doesn't unravel very much when it's cut.

1 Cut a strip of cardboard about 3 cm (1 1/4 in.) wide and 45 cm (18 in.) long. Staple it along the wrong side of one edge of the fabric. Fold over the cardboard and fabric and staple it again.

2 Decorate the fabric with fun designs using glitter glue or markers. Allow the glue to dry.

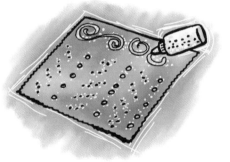

3 Make a wind sock (cylindrical) shape by slightly overlapping and stapling the cardboard ends and gluing together the long sides. Allow the glue to dry.

4 Punch four evenly-spaced holes around the cardboard end. Cut four lengths of string about 100 cm (39 in.) long. Thread one through each hole and knot all eight ends together. (You can staple the string in place instead.) On the other end, use scissors or pinking shears to cut a fringe.

Glue-together puppet

Use thick craft glue for this puppet. It is also helpful if the felt is real rather than acrylic. Use the pattern you create to make many puppets and put on a play.

1 Place your hand on the paper and draw a wide outline around your hand and wrist. Make sure the bottom is very wide.

2 Cut out this paper pattern.

You will need

paper, a pencil, scissors and all-purpose craft glue

felt

buttons and other materials for a face (see step 7)

3 Trace your pattern twice onto the felt with a pencil. (Use chalk or a dried sliver of soap if your felt is a dark color.)

4 Cut out the two felt shapes.

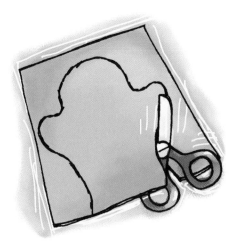

6 Glue the puppet shapes together around the edges.

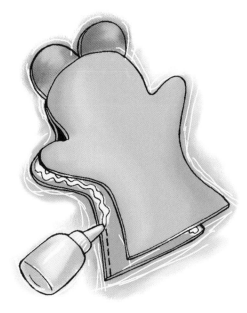

5 If your puppet needs ears or eyes that stick out above the head, cut them out and glue them to one of the puppet shapes.

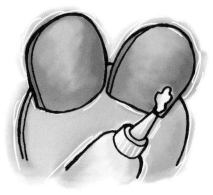

7 Glue on items such as roly eyes, buttons, beads, yarn and other colors of felt to create the face and other features.

Lunch-bag puppet

Use a square-bottomed lunch bag for this fun puppet.

1 Draw a face on the bag in the area shown.

2 Open the bag and stuff the head with two crumpled sheets of paper. Tie a piece of ribbon or yarn loosely around the neck.

3 Cut some strands of yarn and glue them to the head for hair. Add other details if you wish.

4 Tear or cut a hole on each side of the puppet, just under the neck. Put your thumb and baby finger in these holes to make puppet arms. Your other three fingers should fit in the head so you can make your puppet move.

You will need

a paper lunch bag

crayons or markers

2 sheets of scrap paper

ribbon (optional)

yarn

scissors and all-purpose craft glue

MORE IDEAS

Dog puppet

Draw a face on the folded-over bottom of the bag. The fold will be the mouth. Cut out a pink or red construction-paper tongue. Glue it under the fold so it looks like a panting dog. Cut out ears, a collar and a dog tag and glue them in place. Draw on eyes and a nose. Put in your hand and position it so you can open and close the dog's mouth.

Funny bunny puppet

From the inside, use a pencil to poke out two holes in the bottom of the bag. From the outside, cut or tear these holes so they are each large enough to fit your fingers. Draw a bunny face on the front of the bag, and draw or glue on other features. Put your hand inside and poke two fingers through the holes. Make your funny bunny's ears wiggle! Try making an elephant puppet with your finger as the trunk or a giraffe with your fingers as the horns.

Folded frog puppet

Once you've made this funny frog, fold sheets of different-colored paper into different characters. Can you make a dragon? A dog? A rabbit?

1 Fold the sheet of paper lengthwise into thirds. Now fold it in half so the open ends are together.

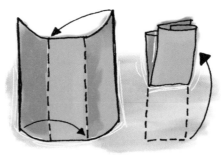

2 Undo this last fold, and then fold each open end to the center fold. Fold the paper in half again so the open ends are now on the top and bottom, facing outwards, and the paper zigzags.

3 Glue the cotton balls on the top. Glue the roly eyes to the front of the cotton balls or draw on eyes. Cut out a red tongue and glue it in place.

4 To make your puppet talk, slip your fingers in the top open end and your thumb in the bottom open end.

You will need

a sheet of green construction paper

2 cotton balls

all-purpose craft glue

2 large roly eyes or a marker

scissors

scraps of fabric or construction paper

Sock dragon

Try making other sock puppets, such as a horse, a cat or any other animal your sock looks like.

1 Turn the sock inside out. Fasten a rubber band around the toe area. Turn the sock right side out.

2 Put your hand inside the sock so your thumb goes in the heel and your fingers are in the foot area. This will create the mouth and give you an idea of where you'd like the eyes, ears and spikes to go. Remove your hand.

3 To make spikes along the back, pull up small areas of the sock and fasten them with rubber bands.

4 Glue on the roly eyes.

5 From the felt, cut out long, thin triangular ears. Glue them in place.

6 Cut out a long, forked tongue and glue it in the mouth.

You will need

a clean adult sock

4 or more thin rubber bands

roly eyes

scraps of felt

scissors and all-purpose craft glue

Jar-lid marionette

Peanut butter or mayonnaise lids are a good size to use for this funny character. Use masking tape or cloth tape rather than clear tape.

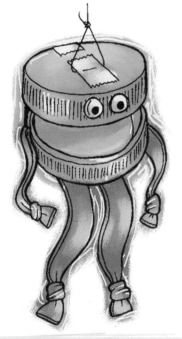

1 Place the two lids upside down on the table so they are touching. Tape them together to create a hinge.

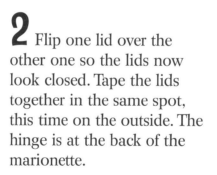

You will need

2 plastic jar lids the same size

masking tape

large roly eyes

all-purpose craft glue and scissors

a square of felt

thread or fishing line

2 Flip one lid over the other one so the lids now look closed. Tape the lids together in the same spot, this time on the outside. The hinge is at the back of the marionette.

3 Glue the eyes to the front of the top lid.

4 Cut four strips of felt from the square.

5 Tape or glue two strips to the underside of the bottom lid for legs. Tape or glue a strip on each side of the same lid to make arms.

6 Make a knot near the end of each strip to make hands and feet. Trim the ends if they're too long.

7 Cut a piece of fishing line. Knot a loop into each end. Tape one loop to the top of the top lid. Put your finger in the other loop to make your marionette talk.

Dancing marionette

For a stick, use a new, unsharpened pencil, a twig, a piece of narrow dowel or any other stick you have around.

1 Flip over the paper plate and draw on a face.

2 See page 28 for how to make construction-paper springs. Make four springs and glue them on for arms and legs.

3 Punch two holes near the top of the plate. Tie a piece of yarn from each hole to the stick and make your marionette dance!

You will need

a paper plate

crayons or markers

construction paper

scissors and all-purpose craft glue or a glue stick

a hole punch

yarn

a stick

Hummingbird

Make a few of these in different colors, and then make them into a mobile.

1 Glue the pom-poms together.

2 Spread glue on the end of a short feather and poke it into the pom-pom for a tail. Glue in longer feathers for the wings.

3 Cut a short piece of pipe cleaner and glue it in place for a beak. Glue on the roly eyes or beads.

4 When the glue is dry, tie fishing line around the hummingbird and hang it up.

You will need

2 medium pom-poms
all-purpose craft glue
craft feathers
a pipe cleaner
roly eyes or beads
fishing line or thread

MORE IDEAS

Sticks are terrific for making mobiles. Use twine or yarn to fasten two sticks together in an "X" shape. Hang these hummingbirds, shells, cones, leaves and other found items from the sticks.

Plastic-bottle bowling game

If you find your plastic-bottle bowling pins fall over too easily, use stones, marbles or dried beans to put a little weight in them.

1 Decorate the bottles with dimensional fabric paint, stickers or permanent markers.

2 Set up the bottles in a straight line or in a triangular pattern.

3 To play the game, use masking tape or a length of yarn to make a line on the floor for bowlers to stand behind. Each player gets three tries to knock over all the pins. Have fun!

You will need

3 or more clean plastic soda or water bottles

supplies for decorating (see step 1)

masking tape or yarn

a ball

Bead-toss game

Use scraps of wrapping paper, construction paper or colorful magazine pictures to cover the writing on the yogurt cup.

1 Glue cut-up scraps of colorful paper on the yogurt cup to decorate it.

2 Turn the cup upside down and use the nail to poke a hole in the center of the bottom.

3 Thread a 50 cm (20 in.) ribbon or string through the hole from the bottom to the inside. Knot the ribbon so it can't come out. Knot the bead on the other end.

4 Toss the bead into the air and catch it in the cup. How many times in a row can you catch it?

You will need

scraps of colorful paper

scissors, all-purpose craft glue and a ruler

a small, clean plastic yogurt cup

a nail

narrow ribbon or heavy string

a large bead

Flash cards

After you've made these flash cards for the alphabet, try simple words or numbers.

1 Write each letter of the alphabet on its own card in capital and small letters.

2 Go through the catalogs and magazines to find and cut out pictures of things that begin with each letter of the alphabet.

3 Glue each picture onto the back of the matching letter card.

4 Quiz your family and friends to see if they can guess the right letter for each picture.

You will need

small index cards

crayons or markers

old catalogs and magazines

scissors and all-purpose craft glue or a glue stick

Memory game

Use old catalogs and magazines to find good pictures for your memory cards. If you don't have recipe or index cards, use squares of thin cardboard.

1 Cut out pairs of small pictures of things that are similar, for example, two pictures of clocks, dolls, birds or cars. Cut out about 20 pairs.

2 Cut the index cards in half and glue the pictures onto them.

3 To make it easier to pick up these thin cards, it's best to play this game on a floor with a carpet. Mix up the cards and place them face down in rows. The first player turns over two cards. If the cards match, she takes the pair. If the cards do not match, she turns them back over. The other players try to remember where the matching cards are so when they have a turn, they will be able to find a matching pair. The player with the most pairs of cards at the end of the game wins.

You will need

old catalogs and magazines

scissors and all-purpose craft glue or a glue stick

index cards about 7.5 cm x 13 cm (3 in. x 5 in.)

127 ⭐

Catalog mix and match

Old catalogs are lots of fun for cut and paste crafts.

1 Cut out pictures of babies, children and adults.

2 Cut out lots of hats, shoes, boots, sports equipment and other things to wear.

3 Mix everything up on the sheets of paper. Glue a huge pair of boots onto a girl in a bathing suit. Give a boy in sports clothing the head of a baby. Put a woman in a business suit on a playground slide. Make up lots of silly combinations.

You will need

old catalogs

scissors and all-purpose craft glue

sheets of paper

Puzzles

Sports and wildlife magazines often have full-page pictures that are fun to make into puzzles. Calendar pictures are great, too.

1 Glue all areas of the picture onto the paper.

2 On the back of the paper, draw curvy lines to create pieces of the puzzle. Cut along the lines.

3 It's best to put this type of puzzle together on a smooth table or counter rather than on a carpet. Store the puzzle pieces in the envelope.

You will need

a large picture

heavy paper

all-purpose craft glue or a glue stick, a pencil and scissors

an envelope

MORE IDEAS

To make your puzzle more challenging, glue a picture onto each side of the paper. It will get confusing trying to figure out which side of the puzzle piece to use.

Marble maze

You'll need lots of cardboard rolls for this craft. After you've made your maze, decorate it with stickers, markers or crayons.

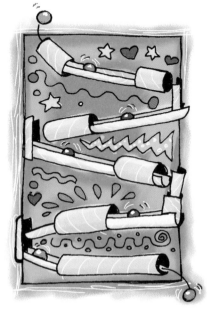

1 Cut the rolls into different sizes and shapes.

2 Lay the rolls on the large cardboard so that they are all slanted slightly downward. Each roll should empty into the next roll.

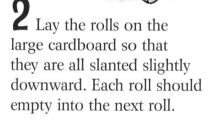

3 Glue the rolls in place. Allow the glue to dry.

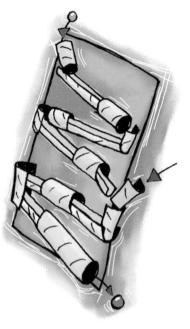

4 Prop the maze against a wall and test it with a marble. If a marble jumps out of the maze, glue or tape on pieces of rolls to fix it.

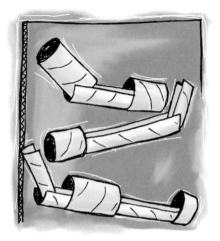

You will need

cardboard rolls

scissors and all-purpose craft glue or tape

a large piece of corrugated cardboard

marbles

stickers, markers or crayons (optional)

Fishing game

For the fishing rod, use a stick, ruler, unsharpened pencil or whatever else you can find.

1 Cut two slits opposite each other in one end of a roll. Cut a triangle of construction paper and slide it into these slits to make a tail.

2 Punch holes around the other end of the roll. Draw on eyes, fins and other markings. Make more fish.

3 Open the paper clip and shape it as shown. Tie it onto one end of the yarn. Tie the other end of the yarn to the rod stick.

4 Go fishing! See if you can hook a fish through one of the holes.

You will need

small cardboard rolls
scissors
construction paper
a hole punch
crayons or markers
a paper clip
yarn or string
a stick

Bubble blower and bubble mixture

If you find it difficult to make bubbles or they don't last long, add 5 mL (1 tsp.) glycerin (available at a drugstore) to the bubble mixture. You can also use store-bought bubble liquid.

1 Twist a petal shape in the wire about 15 cm (6 in.) from one end.

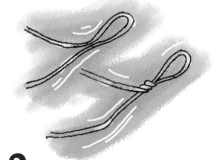

2 Using the longer end of the wire, make another petal shape beside the first one.

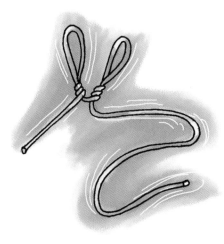

3 Keep making petals until you have five or six. The center of the flower may be a jumble of wire, but that's okay.

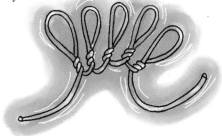

4 When you have enough petals, twist the leftover wire together with the piece you left at the beginning. Cut off any extra wire.

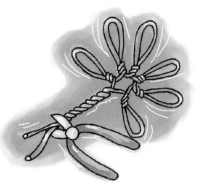

You will need

1 m (1 yd.) of 20-gauge wire (available at hardware stores)

wirecutters or old scissors

assorted beads with large holes

a margarine tub with a lid

50 mL (1/4 c.) dishwashing liquid

50 mL (1/4 c.) water

5 Thread on enough beads to cover about half of the handle. Bend up the wire ends and tuck them into the beads.

7 In the plastic tub, mix together the dishwashing liquid and water.

6 To keep the beads at the lower end of the bubble blower, bend a kink in the wire just above the beads.

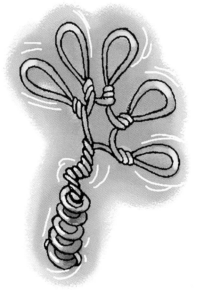

8 Dip the flower into the bubble mixture. Sweep the blower through the air, or blow gently for huge bubbles and blow hard for small ones.

Sock sack

You're sure to have at least one sock with holes in it. That sock is perfect for making this drawstring sock sack to hold your small treasures.

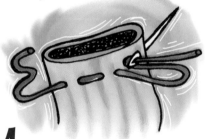

1 Turn the sock inside out. Cut off the foot part of the sock just above the heel. Fasten the cut edge of the sock closed with the rubber band. Cut a piece of yarn, double it and knot it tightly around the rubber band. Trim off the ends of the yarn.

2 Turn the sock right side out. If the sock is plain, you may wish to decorate it. Place a small piece of cardboard inside the sock. Decorate one side, allow it to dry, then decorate the other side. Or stitch or glue buttons or beads onto the sock. Discard the cardboard

3 Thread yarn into the large needle. Weave a row of stitches about 2.5 cm (1 in.) below the open end of the sock. Pull the yarn out of the needle, knot the ends together and trim off the extra yarn.

4 Starting at the opposite side of the sock, make another row of stitches just below the first row. To close the sack, pull the yarn ends in opposite directions.

Jingle-bell instrument

Check the index at the back of this book for more musical instruments to make.

1 Thread a bell onto the pipe cleaner so it is near the end.

2 Bend the pipe cleaner and twist the bell twice. Straighten the pipe cleaner.

3 Thread on as many bells as you can fit, twisting each one on the pipe cleaner to hold it in place.

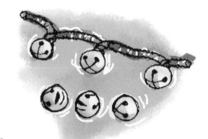

4 Twist the ends of the pipe cleaner together to make a circle. If the pipe-cleaner ends feel sharp, wind some tape around them.

You will need

5 or more jingle bells

a pipe cleaner

tape (optional)

Paper-plate shaker

This instrument is part shaker, part drum and part tambourine. Strike up the band!

1 Glue a few streamers to the edge of one of the paper plates.

2 In this same plate, place the beans and the bells (if you are using bells).

3 Glue the other plate face down onto the first one. Allow the glue to dry.

4 Decorate both sides of the shaker using markers, crayons, stickers, tissue paper or other items.

You will need

streamers, ribbon or strips of tissue paper

2 paper plates

all-purpose craft glue

beans, beads or pebbles

2 or more jingle bells (optional)

supplies for decorating (see step 4)

Water-bottle shaker

Put a couple of bells in your shaker along with the beads to get a nice jingling sound.

1 Take off the lid and drop beads into the bottle. Fasten the lid closed and give it a shake. Add or take away beads to get the sound you like.

2 Open the bottle again and spread glue around the neck of the bottle. Close the lid tightly and allow the glue to dry.

3 Wind a strip of tape (you may need to cut or tear the tape to make it narrower) around the lid to secure it.

You will need

a clean, clear, dry water bottle

an assortment of small, colorful beads

2 or more jingle bells (optional)

all-purpose craft glue

strong cloth or duct tape

Marching-band drum

For this drum you can use any plastic tub, from a small yogurt cup to a large ice-cream pail. Then join the marching band.

1 Drape the ribbon around your neck. Cut it a little longer than where you'd like your drum to hang.

2 Make a knot in each end of the ribbon. Open the plastic tub and place the knotted ends inside, across from each other. Close the lid.

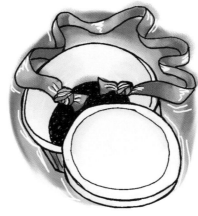

3 If you like, you can decorate the drum with stickers, cutout pictures or drawings using non-toxic permanent markers. It is best to keep the lid undecorated.

4 For drumsticks, use the eraser ends of the pencils. Or use other sticks with a ball of tape or a large bead on one end. Drum roll, please!

You will need

ribbon

scissors

a clean plastic tub with a lid

supplies for decorating (see step 3)

2 unsharpened pencils with erasers or other sticks with tape or beads

DECORATE and CELEBRATE

Decorating eggs

You can decorate eggs that are hard-boiled or blown out. Here's how to prepare each type of egg. Read on for lots of decorating ideas.

Hard-boiled eggs

Place the eggs in a pot and cover them completely with water. Put the lid on the pot. Ask an adult to bring the eggs to a boil, remove the pot from the heat and let it stand for 20 minutes. When the time is up, cool the eggs thoroughly in cold water. Dry them off and decorate them. Decorated hard-boiled eggs can be eaten in a day or two as long as they have been kept refrigerated. If you wish to keep the eggs for display only, they will be fine for a couple of weeks in a basket.

Blown-out eggs

Eggs will need to be blown out by an adult. Thoroughly wash and dry each egg. Use a long darning needle to poke a small hole in each end. To make it easier to blow out the yolk, poke the needle farther into one end to break the yolk. Blow the contents of the egg into a small bowl. Rinse out the shell with water and blow it out. Dry off the egg and it is ready to be decorated. These eggs are fragile so they need to be handled very gently. They will keep for years and can be stored in an egg carton when they are not on display.

Decorating ideas

You can display your fancy eggs in egg cups or a basket or on small bottle lids. You can make stands by cutting sections off a cardboard roll or taping a strip of construction paper into a small circle.

Dyed eggs: To get nice pastel colors, stir food coloring into a mixture of equal amounts of water and vinegar. Dip white eggs into the mixture and set them in a cup or carton or on a paper towel to dry.

Drawn on and dyed eggs: Draw a design or message on a white egg with a white crayon. Dye the egg as described above.

Painted eggs: You can paint eggs with watercolor paint, acrylic craft paint or dimensional fabric paint. Allow the egg to dry on a stand or in a cup. Instead of using paint, you can draw on eggs with markers.

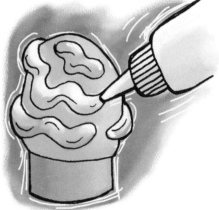

Sponge-painted eggs: Use a small piece of a sponge to dab acrylic craft paint all over an egg. Allow it to dry, then sponge another color over top. Or, cut a small square or rectangle of sponge, dip it in paint and create designs on an egg.

Button bouquet

Here's a chance to use some of those extra-large buttons from the button box.

1 Fold a pipe cleaner in half. Thread on a button so it sits at the bent end of the pipe cleaner.

2 Twist the folded pipe cleaner together all the way down its length.

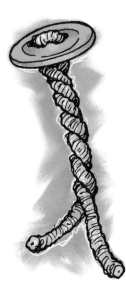

3 To make leaves, twist a green pipe cleaner around the stem. Shape the ends into leaves.

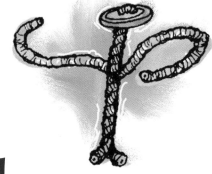

4 Make more button flowers. Tie them together with a ribbon if you like or place them in a vase.

You will need

pipe cleaners
large buttons
ribbon (optional)

Fuzzy flowers

These instructions are for making one flower, but once you've made one, you'll want to make a whole bouquet!

1 Wind a pipe cleaner around the pencil so it looks like a spring.

2 Slide the pipe cleaner off the pencil and stretch it out a little. Hook and twist the ends together to form a coiled circle.

3 Bend the second pipe cleaner in half. Hook it through the flower. Tightly twist it down its entire length to form the stem.

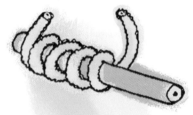

4 For the leaves, twist the third pipe cleaner around the stem as if you were fastening on a twist tie. Shape the ends into leaves.

You will need

3 pipe cleaners

an unsharpened pencil or a pen with a lid

Giant tissue flower

You can use a giant tissue flower as a bow on a gift, or make a bouquet to use as decoration for a party.

1 Hold the two pipe cleaners side-by-side and twist them together. Thread the bead on one end and bend the pipe cleaners to hold the bead in place.

2 Cut out about ten large tissue-paper circles, each about the size of a lunch plate. (The circles do not need to be perfect.) You can cut the circles so the edges are smooth, wavy, pointed, or you can make cuts into the edges.

3 Stick a small square of tape on the center of the first flower shape you are going to use. Poke the pipe-cleaner ends through the tape and slide the flower up to the bead.

4 Slide the other tissue shapes onto the pipe cleaners. Push all the layers of tissue upward and pinch them together at the base of the flower. Hold this shape by fastening on a small piece of pipe cleaner. You should still be able to see the bead in the center of the flower.

You will need

2 1/4 pipe cleaners

a big bead with a large hole

colorful tissue paper

scissors

masking tape

Tissue-paper butterfly

To display your butterfly, you can stick on a magnet and put it on the fridge or tie a string on it and hang it up. If you make a few butterflies in different colors, you could make a butterfly mobile (see page 123).

1 Cut out three rectangles of different-colored tissue, each about 15 cm x 20 cm (6 in. x 8 in.). Gather all three rectangles together in the center to make a bow.

2 Open the clothespin and pinch the gathered tissue paper inside it.

3 Bend the pipe cleaner in half and curl the ends to make antennae. Pinch the antennae in the clothespin, too. Add a dab of glue.

4 Glue a strip of tissue paper on the clothespin to cover it. For extra sparkle, hold the butterfly over a sheet of paper. Dot glue on the wings, sprinkle on glitter and gently shake off the extra glitter.

You will need

colorful tissue paper

a ruler, scissors and all-purpose craft glue

a clothespin with a spring

half a tinsel pipe cleaner

paper and glitter (optional)

Paper-plate pouch

Use this handy pouch for postcards and greeting cards
or fill it with flowers you've made from the instructions in this book.

1 Cut one of the paper plates in half. Punch about 12 holes evenly around its outside edge.

2 Place the half plate on the whole plate and use the pencil to mark where each hole should be made on the whole plate. Punch out the marked holes.

You will need

2 paper plates

a hole punch

scissors, a pencil and tape

yarn

crayon, markers or stickers

3 Cut a piece of yarn twice the length of an adult's arm. Wrap a little tape around one end.

4 Place the half plate on the whole plate again and line up the holes. Thread the taped end of the yarn through the first set of holes. Tie the untaped end in this hole. Leave a tail on the knot.

6 When you reach the end of the holes, sew back again to where you first started. Tie the yarn to the tail you left on the knot at the beginning. Cut the yarn and tuck the ends inside the pouch.

7 Punch two holes at the top of the whole plate. Thread a piece of yarn through them and knot the yarn ends together.

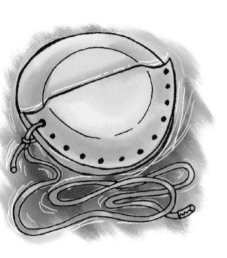

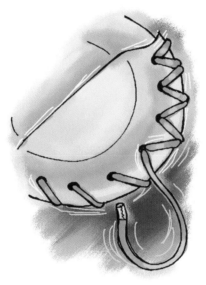

8 Decorate your pouch. Hang it on a nail, bulletin board or your doorknob.

5 "Sew" the plates together using the taped end of the yarn as a needle.

Paper-bag basket

Use a square-bottomed paper bag, any size, for this project. Instead of a twisted paper handle, you can punch a hole in each side and fasten on a pipe cleaner.

1 Cut about one-third off the top of the bag. Twist the strip to make a basket handle.

2 Fold down the top of the bag all around. Smooth it and fold it down again. If there is writing on the bag, you may wish to keep folding down the top until none of the writing shows.

3 Hold the handle in place and trim it if it is too long. Untwist just the ends of the handle so you can staple them to the sides of the bag.

4 Decorate the basket with crayons, markers, eraser prints (see page 20) or stickers. You could also glue on buttons, beads, ribbon, lace or magazine pictures. Use your basket to hold a craft project, some treasures or your picnic lunch.

You will need

a paper bag

scissors

a stapler

supplies for decorating (see step 4)

Lantern

**Put some crumpled yellow tissue paper in the lantern
to make it look like candlelight.**

1 Cut off the front of the card. Fold it in half lengthwise so that the picture shows.

2 Make cuts that start at the folded edge but stop before the opposite edge.

3 Unfold the card and glue the ends together. Hold the glued area for a moment while it dries.

4 For a handle, cut a strip from the back of the card or from another card front. Glue the ends across the inside of the top of the lantern.

You will need

a used greeting card

*scissors and
all-purpose craft glue
or a glue stick*

Sparkly paper chain

Make your paper chain as long as you like. You can make a plain chain if you don't have glitter.

1 Place a sheet of construction paper on the waxed paper. Squirt glue all over it in lines and swirls.

2 Sprinkle glitter over the glue. Shake the sheet a little to make sure all the glue is covered. Shake the extra glitter onto the waxed paper.

3 Set aside the glittery paper to dry. Lift the sides of the waxed paper to form a trough and pour the extra glitter back into the container. Prepare other sheets of different-colored construction paper.

4 When the sheets are dry, cut them into narrow strips. Glue one strip into a circle. Slip another strip through the circle, and glue that strip into a circle, too. Keep going until you've used all the strips.

You will need

a sheet of waxed paper

construction paper

all-purpose craft glue

glitter

scissors

Cookie-cutter decorations

Use markers, crayons, fabric and paper scraps, buttons, beads, yarn, ribbon and other trim to decorate your cutout.

1 Trace a cookie cutter twice onto the construction paper. Cut out both shapes.

2 Spread glue all over one side of one of the shapes.

3 Cut a piece of floss or thread and fold it in half. Place the ends in the glue and place the other cookie-cutter shape over top.

4 Decorate one or both sides. Use your cutout for a decoration or gift tag. Make lots more!

You will need

cookie cutters

construction paper

a pencil, scissors and all-purpose craft glue

embroidery floss or thread

supplies for decorating

Beaded star

Once you've made this star, try using white beads on white or blue pipe cleaners to make a snowflake.

1 Cut both pipe cleaners in half. Set one half piece aside for a different project.

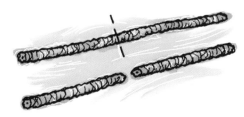

2 Hold the three pipe-cleaner pieces so the ends are even. Twist them together in the center. Spread the pipe cleaners apart to make a star shape.

3 Thread beads on one point of the star. Fold over the end of the pipe cleaner to keep the beads in place. Bead the other five points the same way.

4 To hang up your star, tie thread or fishing line on one of the points. It looks nice in a window.

You will need

2 pipe cleaners
scissors
sparkling beads
thread or fishing line

Paper cones

Make a bunch of these and fill them with small treats. You can also make them in seasonal colors and hang them from a Christmas tree.

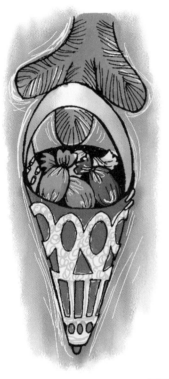

1 Glue the paper doily onto the construction paper. Allow it to dry, then cut it out.

2 Fold the circle in half, open it and cut it in half along the fold line. Set aside one half to make into a second cone when you finish the first one.

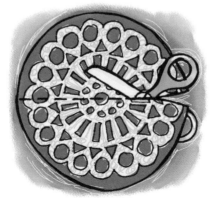

3 Glue or staple the half-circle into a cone shape.

4 Cut a strip of construction paper for a handle and glue or staple it in place.

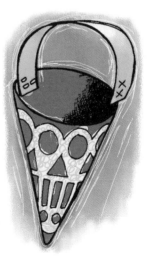

You will need

a round paper doily

scissors and all-purpose craft glue or a glue stick

construction paper

a stapler (optional)

Snowflakes

Make a variety of sizes of snowflakes by tracing cups, bowls, saucers and plastic tubs onto almost any type of paper.

1 Trace circles onto the paper and cut them out.

2 Fold each circle in half and then in thirds.

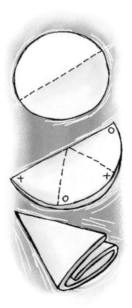

3 Cut out pieces from the folded circles as shown. Open them to find one-of-a-kind snowflakes.

4 If you like, you can spread a bit of glue on a snowflake and sprinkle on glitter. Tape the snowflakes to windows or walls or tie on thread and hang them on doorknobs, ceilings or archways.

You will need

paper

cups or bowls to trace

a pencil and scissors

all-purpose craft glue and glitter (optional)

Candy-cane reindeer

Don't eat all the candy canes — save one for this whimsical reindeer. You can hang it up or give it as a gift.

1 Twist the pipe cleaner around the crook of the candy cane. Bend the ends to look like antlers.

2 Glue on a pair of roly eyes.

3 Glue on a pom-pom nose. Allow the glue to dry.

You will need

a candy cane

a pipe cleaner

a pair of roly eyes

a tiny red pom-pom or bead

all-purpose craft glue

Doily angel

This angel can stand on its own or be hung up if you tie fishing line or yarn from the halo.

1 Glue the paper doily onto the construction paper. Allow it to dry, then cut it out.

You will need

a paper doily about 13 cm (5 in.) in diameter

construction paper

scissors and a glue stick or all-purpose craft glue

a stapler

a tinsel or regular pipe cleaner

a wooden bead

paint and a brush or markers

yarn or fishing line (optional)

2 Fold the doily circle in half, open it and cut it along the fold line.

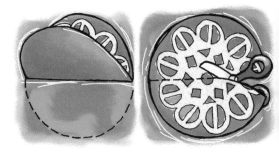

3 Staple one of the halves into a cone shape. Set aside the other half for the angel wings.

4 Make a small circle halo in the center of the pipe cleaner as shown. Thread the bead onto the pipe-cleaner ends. Bend the halo so it sits on the bead head.

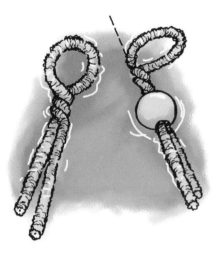

5 Poke the pipe-cleaner ends into the small hole in the pointed end of the cone. Staple one or both pipe-cleaner ends to the inside of the cone. Trim the ends if they stick out past the bottom of your angel's dress.

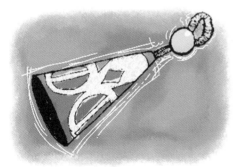

6 Trim off a little of the straight edge of the doily wings. Glue or staple them to the back of the angel.

7 Draw or paint on an angel face.

8 If you'd like your angel to have hair, cut a few strands of yarn and tie them loosely around the base of the halo. Style the hair if you wish.

Glitter and glue ornaments

Use thick craft glue for these ornaments, but not tacky glue. It stays too soft.

1 Hold the nozzle of the glue bottle above the waxed paper and draw simple designs with glue. Try a circle, a diamond, a star or an icicle.

2 If the glue is uneven, smooth it out a little with a toothpick.

You will need

a waxed-paper lined cookie sheet

all-purpose craft glue

glitter

a toothpick

a needle and thread or fishing line

3 Sprinkle glitter all over the designs so you cannot see any glue. Leave the extra glitter on the design.

4 Set the tray in a warm spot to dry overnight.

5 If the ornaments are dry, they should lift easily off the waxed paper. If the ornaments are still stuck, allow more drying time.

6 When your ornaments are dry, it is optional to spread a thin layer of glue on the back of each one and sprinkle on a little more glitter. Allow them to dry again.

7 To hang up your ornaments, poke through them with a needle and thread or fishing line. Cut the thread and tie the ends into a knot.

Greeting-card ornament

For a festive look, use seasonal greeting cards and dip the edges of the ornament in glue, then glitter.

1 Fold a length of embroidery floss about 40 cm (16 in.) long in half and set it aside.

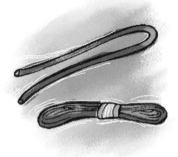

2 Use the cup to trace five circles onto colorful areas of the cards. Cut them out.

3 Fold each circle in half so the picture is on the inside.

you will need

embroidery floss

used greeting cards

a cup

pencil, scissors, a ruler and all-purpose craft glue

4 Spread glue on one of the plain halves of one of the folded circles. Press half of another folded circle onto the glued area.

6 Run a line of glue down the center area. Place the folded floss in it so the ends are in the glue and the looped end is free.

7 Glue the last folded circle in place to close the ornament. Allow the glue to dry before you hang up the ornament.

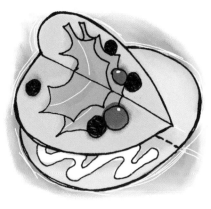

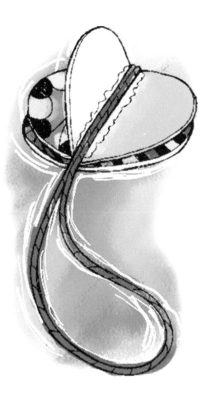

5 Apply glue to the other half of the second circle and press on a third circle. Then glue on the fourth circle.

Woven yarn ornament

**Variegated yarn has many colors on one ball.
It's great for this type of weaving.**

1 Cross the sticks and hold the end of the yarn in the center of the cross. Wind the yarn in both diagonal directions to cover the yarn end and hold the sticks together.

2 Position the cross so it is straight up and down. Tightly wind the yarn once behind and around the stick on the right side.

3 Turn the cross in a clockwise direction as you bring the yarn behind and around the next stick.

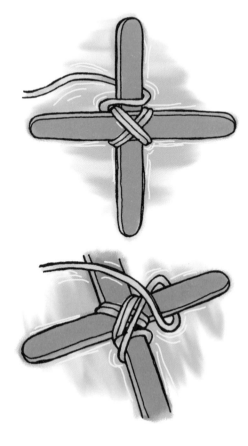

You will need

*2 Popsicle sticks
variegated yarn
scissors*

4 Keep turning the cross and tightly winding the yarn around each stick. Do not overlap the yarn.

5 When you run out of space, cut the yarn leaving a long tail.

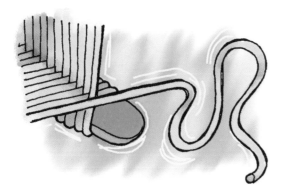

6 Tuck the yarn end under the last strand of yarn on the diamond to the right of the Popsicle stick. Thread it through the loop as shown. Pull the tail upward so the knot ends up behind the stick.

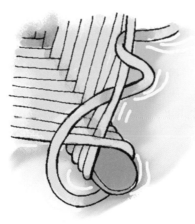

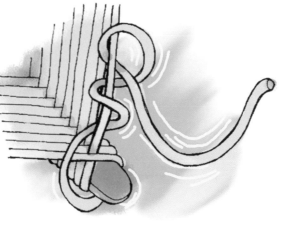

7 Repeat step 6. Use the yarn end to hang up your woven design. It will turn so you can see how beautiful the other side is, too.

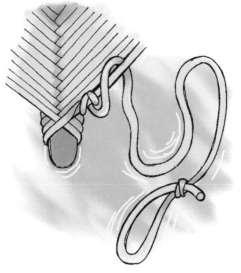

Tissue stained glass

Try this with a simple design, such as a heart, a large flower or the moon and stars.

1 Draw shapes onto one of the sheets of construction paper. Poke the scissors into the center of each shape so you can cut it out.

3 On one sheet of construction paper, glue a piece of tissue paper over each cutout.

2 Hold the two sheets of paper together and trace the cutout shapes onto the uncut construction paper. Cut them out, too.

4 Glue the two sheets together, matching all the cutouts. Hang your tissue stained glass in a window.

You will need

a pencil, scissors and all-purpose craft glue

2 sheets of construction paper

pieces of colorful tissue paper

Paper cutouts

Try different color combinations for this neat craft.
Make miniatures for gift tags and decorations.

1 Fold one sheet of paper in half, and then in half again. Or fold it any way you like.

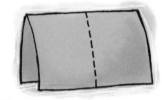

2 Cut away pieces of the folded paper. Open it.

3 Glue it onto the other sheet of construction paper.

You will need

2 different-colored sheets of construction paper

scissors

all-purpose craft glue or a glue stick

Valentine doily

Make a whole batch of these so you can give your family
and friends pretty handmade valentines.

1 Fold a piece of
construction paper in half.
Along the fold line, draw
and cut out half a heart.

2 Open the heart and glue
it on the doily.

3 If you like, you can glue
on another heart to decorate
the valentine and write on a
message.

you will need

*red or pink
construction paper*

*scissors and
all-purpose craft glue
or a glue stick*

a paper doily

markers or crayons

plain paper (optional)

Folded-paper puppy card

After making this puppy, try making a pig with a large two-hole button for the nose.

You will need

a sheet of paper

crayons or markers, scissors and all-purpose craft glue or a glue stick

roly eyes (optional)

construction paper

1 To make a square, fold the top end of the sheet of paper so it is even with the left side. Cut off the strip along the bottom. Keep the square folded diagonally.

2 Position the triangle as shown. Fold up the bottom point, then fold it and glue it back down to make a nose. Color the nose.

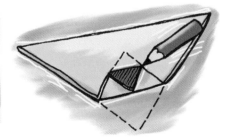

3 Fold down the other two points to make ears. Draw or glue on eyes. Color in other markings.

4 Fold a sheet of construction paper in half and glue the puppy to it. Write a message inside, such as "Have a doggone good birthday."

Folded-paper tiger card

You can make a mini tiger by using a small square of paper. Glue it onto a Popsicle stick to make a puppet.

1 To make a square, follow step 1 on page 167. Keep the square folded diagonally.

2 Bend down the top of the triangle so the tip ends up about halfway down the triangle.

3 Bend up the other two corners to make ears. Flip the shape over and adjust the ears until they look just right.

4 Draw on a face and tiger stripes. Fold the construction paper in half and glue the tiger to the front of it. Glue half a sheet of white paper inside so you can write on a message, such as "Go wild on your birthday!"

You will need

paper

crayons or markers, scissors and all-purpose craft glue or a glue stick

a sheet of construction paper

Yarn greetings

Stitch up a simple greeting card for someone special.

1 Fold together the two sheets of construction paper.

2 Open the sheets, keep them together and punch holes evenly all around the four sides.

3 Cut a length of yarn about three times the length of an adult's arm. Wind a little tape around one end of the yarn.

4 Leave a yarn tail in the bottom right corner of the card and stitch it all around. When you get back to where you started, tie the yarn ends into a bow. Decorate the card and write a message in it.

You will need

2 sheets of different-colored construction paper

a hole punch

yarn

tape

crayons or markers

Blooming paper

Glue this pretty paper flower in a picture or on the front of a card.

1 Trace three different-sized circles onto the construction paper and cut them out.

2 Make cuts part way into each circle, all the way around to form petals.

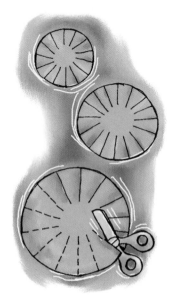

3 On each circle, bend and curl the petals by rolling them up or by wrapping them around your pencil.

4 Glue the largest circle in place first, then the middle one and then the smallest. Draw a center in the flower or glue on a button or bead. Draw a stem and leaves or cut them out of construction paper.

You will need

cups, plastic tubs and lids to trace

construction paper

a pencil, scissors and all-purpose craft glue or a glue stick

markers, crayons, a button or a bead (optional)

Party favors

For your next birthday party, make a bunch of these and give them out instead of loot bags. See page 173 for how to make a gift tag to attach to your party favor.

1 Cover one end of the roll with a small piece of wrapping paper. Hold the paper in place with the rubber band.

2 Fill the roll with treats, such as wrapped candies, plastic animals, stickers, crayons or craft supplies.

3 Wrap the roll with a strip of wrapping paper so there is extra paper on each end. Tape the paper in place, leaving the ends open.

4 Tie a piece of ribbon at each end of the roll to close it.

You will need

a cardboard roll

wrapping paper

scissors

a rubber band

treats (see step 2)

clear tape

ribbon

Greeting-card gift bag

If you don't have used greeting cards, decorate the bag with drawings or stickers.

1 Cut the fronts off the cards.

2 Glue a card to each side of the bag.

3 Place the gift inside and fold down the top of the bag. Punch two holes in the folded area.

4 Thread the ribbon through the holes and tie it in a bow.

You will need

2 used greeting cards

a square-bottomed paper lunch bag

a glue stick

a hole punch

curling ribbon or yarn

Gift tags

These small, shaped cards are perfect for gift tags.
Make them large and use them for greeting cards, too.

1 Fold a piece of construction paper in half. It does not need to be a full sheet.

2 Draw a cookie-cutter shape on the paper, with part of the shape against the folded edge.

3 Cut it out, leaving the folded edge, and decorate it with markers or crayons. Write your message inside.

You will need

construction paper
cookie cutters
a pencil and scissors
markers or crayons

Index

You can use this index to find projects that use specific materials (for example, egg cartons) or to find particular kinds of projects (for example, decorations or puppets).